SPECIAL
General e
Associate   Pumfrey and
Sheila W

Inclusi

Related titles:

Julia Anghileri: *Teaching Number Sense*
Peter Benton and Tim O'Brien: *Special Needs and the Beginning Teacher*
Paul Croll and Diana Moses: *Special Needs in the Primary School*
Julie Dockrell and David Messer: *Children's Language and Communication Difficulties*
Marilyn Nickson: *Teaching and Learning Mathematics*
Adrian Oldknow and Ron Taylor: *Teaching Maths with ICT*
Brian Robbins: *Inclusive Mathematics 5–11*

Inclusive Mathematics 11–18

Mike Ollerton and Anne Watson

CONTINUUM
London and New York

Continuum

The Tower Building
11 York Road
London SE1 7NX

370 Lexington Avenue
New York
New York 10017-6503

First published 2001

British Library Cataloguing-in-Publication Data
A catalogue record for this book is available from the British Library.

ISBN 0-8264-5201-9

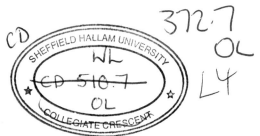
Typeset by BookEns Ltd, Royston, Herts
Printed and bound in Great Britain by
T.J. International Ltd, Padstow, Cornwall

Contents

—1—

Introduction

This book is about methods of teaching mathematics that include all students in the development of mathematical thinking and give access to the whole of the secondary mathematics curriculum. In fact, we think the school curriculum can be limiting, and many of the ideas in the book include curriculum mathematics within a broader view of mathematical learning.

We have been secondary mathematics teachers and heads of department for a total of 37 years, and we both still teach school children from time to time, spend a good deal of time in classrooms and work with experienced teachers as well as beginners. We know about schools, classrooms, teachers and children and understand the real pressures and constraints of schools. We have both worked in well-resourced and poorly-resourced schools, taught a wide range of children with high and low expectations, high and low achievement, special needs of all kinds, from comfortable suburbs and from almost derelict city estates.

Why do we set out our credentials? Because all the ideas in this book are real, tried and tested, and many of them may surprise you. Some of them have been features of our practice for nearly the whole of our careers; others are recent developments; the rest are examples of good teaching that we have seen being used in other people's classrooms. Every idea is usable successfully in ordinary classrooms. By success we mean that, in our experience, children learn mathematics, and enjoy it, and do well in associated assessments.

But this is more than a book of ideas. Indeed, ideas on their own are of limited use. It is possible to have disastrous lessons using some of our ideas; it is possible to have successful lessons using very different approaches to ours. The route to 'successful' varies between lessons and teachers. While writing, we had in mind reflective teachers who may wish to review how they do things, and for whom some of the things we say might be helpful, others challenging, and others candidates for immediate rejection.

Most of our practice arises from some fundamental beliefs about mathematics, students, teaching and learning. By writing about curriculum structure, classroom atmosphere and assessment we provide a context for the lessons and sequences of lessons. Most of all, we are driven by the belief that there are ways to teach, with integrity, mathematics to all children, inclusively. We have done it, and the methods we used have been shown to lead to higher achievement for most students than comparable groups taught conventionally.[1]

INCLUSION

In many of the secondary comprehensive schools founded in the UK in the 1970s, most subjects were taught in mixed-ability groups, often with accompanying developments in the curriculum. Such developments usually focused on the learning skills identified as important in a subject: reading, comprehension, research, group work, communication and understanding. However, even in schools which spoke proudly of a comprehensive ideal, mathematics was usually still taught in groups selected according to some notion of 'ability', students being separated early in secondary school and given differentiated curriculum tracks in 'top sets', 'bottom sets' and 'middle sets'.

In some areas of the country individualized workcard or booklet systems were developed to allow students to learn mathematics in mixed-ability groups by studying, in effect, on their own track from printed resources. In other areas, teachers tried to develop approaches to mixed-ability teaching that allowed all students to share a common starting point but progress in different directions, at different rates, within a topic. At the same time, moves to reconsider the nature of school mathematics were taking place. A new emphasis emerged, less on skills and procedures and more on understanding and thinking mathematically. A view of learning that recognized the individual construction of mathematical meaning and knowledge, rather than mathematics as the successful repetition of taught procedures and facts, grew alongside this approach.

Individualized systems, while recognizing that students all learn at different rates in different ways, do not necessarily take advantage of the variety of different viewpoints in one class, the power of discussion, the pedagogic knowledge of the teacher and the entitlement of each student to access the whole curriculum. The approach we use, of using common starting points with the whole mixed-ability class, allows all students to work on a topic, though this may be understood by students in different ways at different times. It is supported by discussion, group work, and the overt use of the teacher's special knowledge and mathematical expertise. Coupled with more emphasis on the students' constructions of understanding, and the development of their mathematical thinking, the whole class approach allows for mixed-ability teaching in ways which value the contribution and ways of learning of all students, not just the brightest nor just the 'average' student in the group. We have the high, but realistic, expectation that every student can understand something of all concepts taught at secondary level. To shift the emphasis from the acquisition of skills and procedures to the development of understanding requires new approaches to teaching. The nature of the tasks given to students has to change, the purpose of practising algorithms has to be clear, the expectations of the teacher and the students about what it is to be a 'good' student have to change, and the assessment patterns have to change. This shift has taken place in the UK and is, at the time of writing, also taking place elsewhere.

Meanwhile, there has been a general recognition that education can and does lead to outcomes that systematically discriminate between different social groups. Certain racial groups and social classes are advantaged or disadvantaged by different teaching and assessment methods; gendered underachievement in specific school subjects is the focus of much research, debate and experimentation. The 1999 National Curriculum for England (Mathematics) sets out three principles for the development of an inclusive curriculum: setting suitable challenges, responding to diverse needs and overcoming potential barriers to learning and assessment. These issues can be tackled at several levels, from compensatory pre-school education, through community involvement in schools, critical adaptation of school curricula, to affirmative action at entry into higher education. We take a rather different line by looking at what it means to teach and learn mathematics, and attempting to give all students access to the curriculum as it is, within the assessment structure as it is.

This does not mean we are happy as things stand, but it reflects an understanding of the need students, particularly adolescents, have to be successful and enfranchised through whatever paths are available at the time.

REFORMED CURRICULA

In 1988 the introduction of the National Curriculum for England and Wales placed a statutory duty on teachers to change their practice in several ways. All mathematics teachers had to include the use and application of mathematics in the curriculum, and introduce extended tasks for all students, not just those in innovative schools, for the purposes of teaching, learning and assessment. The nature of national test questions changed to include many in which mathematics was contexualized, and some where students had to give reasons, make judgements, or give alternative answers, rather than merely apply algorithms. In these respects, UK curriculum changes were in the vanguard of international changes in mathematics curricula. In general, the term 'reform curriculum' used in other countries indicates the same kinds of change: a recognition that students construct their own understandings of mathematics over time; that there are ways of teaching which capitalize on students' own constructions, rather than expecting all to move in the same direction at the same time; that understanding mathematics cannot necessarily be assessed in timed tests; that application and use of mathematics is a more worthwhile learning outcome than unquestioning performance of algorithms.

The successes and failures of the changes in the UK presaged difficulties in similar innovations elsewhere, and there were many subsequent attempts to legislate for further changes in the mathematics curriculum and teaching methods to take account of differing perceptions of what 'ought' to be the curriculum and the educational outcomes. We shall not go into that story here. Instead we want to make the point that there is a long history in the UK of the development of appropriate, inclusive, teaching methods, pioneered most notably by The Association of Teachers of Mathematics, inspired by Caleb Gattegno, Dick Tahta and others. It is in that tradition we see ourselves.

THE TEXT OF THE BOOK: COMPLEXITIES OF TEACHING

Teaching mathematics is a complex activity. At any one moment in the classroom the teacher has to make decisions about a number of features: mathematics, individual students' needs, problems and progress, the progress of the class as a whole, the timing and pace of the lesson, interactions between students, social dynamics, administrative matters, the imposed curriculum and what to say to each student or the whole class in response to their work. Different writers will give priority to different categories: some to the structuring of the mathematical work, some to the social dynamics of the classroom, some to the quality of verbal interactions and others to the underlying cognitive challenges to the students. All of these have value, and all have inspired (or arisen from) research into mathematics classrooms. In writing a book, one necessarily has to decide what is said, and decide on the order in which it is said. We have chosen to describe practice in general terms first, and then illustrate how some mathematical topics might be taught within such practice. In most chapters we invite the reader to consider some of the issues in relation to their own practice and beliefs. Some of the questions we pose are brief; others require considerable thought. The purpose of them is to recognize the value of your own views and experiences and express these as a context for reading on. It is highly likely that readers will sometimes find themselves agreeing with us, and sometimes disagreeing.

For instance, our interpretation of our teaching experience leads us to believe that students generally learn in a non-linear fashion, and that all students sometimes learn more when plunged into a complex mathematical situation than when taught with a simple-to-complex, step-by-step approach. This can be explained by recognizing that sorting out complex situations, discriminating between their parts, identifying variables and relationships within situations are all natural human abilities. Without the ability to do this people are unable to function well in society; those who cannot do this are diagnosed and given special help. In our teaching we expect students to be able to handle complexity in mathematics, but they may need some help in a supportive environment to succeed, particularly if their previous experiences of mathematics have led them to close down these abilities and wait for simple, linear pathways to be given to them. This is not to say that there is no place for step-by-step approaches, but such places have to be identified and rationalized.

Another feature of our teaching is that we do not rely on 'fun' contexts and 'lesson fillers' to vary the pace of a lesson, to provide practice tasks, and to engender motivation in their lessons. This is not to say that puzzles and games and mathematical fun have no place. Indeed we recognize the need for adolescents to be emotionally attached to their work (a need which may override all other adolescent needs) and we generate involvement through the intrigues and surprises inherent in mathematics, the feeling of success that mathematics can give after a long mental struggle, and an enhanced sense of learning.

Sometimes, when we talk to teachers about our work, we are told, 'I couldn't do that with my students, there would be mayhem!' This makes us realize that another belief we share is in trusting students, all students, to work on what they find interesting and get delight from their progress. The balance between discipline and mathematical work requires pedagogic decisions, and different teachers develop different emphases. Among teachers we admire, some will be quite strict from the start about classroom issues such as listening, being usefully engaged in work, keeping work carefully and so on. Some will not mention behaviour until its negotiation is necessary, while others will never mention it, preferring to wait until involvement in mathematics becomes such a deeply shared task that students are naturally self-disciplined. We know that all these approaches are possible with all groups, though establishment of a working ethos depends also on outside features such as school norms, teaching groups, previous experiences of the students and so on.

Our hope is that readers will not reject any ideas which provoke negative reactions, but will instead consider them seriously in the light of their own work. The chapters also contain many examples of classroom incidents and background stories to which readers will probably want to add their own.

Throughout the book there are mathematical prompts, usually given as examples of teaching approaches. These could be of use to anyone, whatever their reaction to some of our more controversial beliefs and statements. In particular, Chapters 9–14 offer outlines of sequences of lessons on particular secondary topics. Within these chapters we identify teaching strategies in the context of specific topics; such strategies can be extracted and used across the whole curriculum. Most of the mathematical ideas have the potential to be extended well beyond the school curriculum, and we often give indications of how such extension can be prompted. In addition, every topic contains opportunities to practise algorithmic skills and techniques, though this is not always pointed out. We envisage readers deciding how tasks can be used in practice, and how they can be extended.

Note that most tasks we offer can be treated at a mundane level: students could follow instructions mechanically; spatial tasks can become opportunities for merely colouring-in; some students may stick at repetitive stages without taking the risk to generalize from their results. However, through our teaching we expect all students to think mathematically about what they were doing, and we have always found it possible to engender complex, non-elementary thinking. But sometimes repetition and practice, colouring-in to emphasize features and patterns, and working at an automatic, rhythmic pace are useful for all students through providing a context for subconscious working, developing fluency and intuition.

It is our intention, then, that this book should not make light of the challenge teachers face, and not dismiss ways of working other than ours. Instead we hope it will give opportunity to think afresh about many common features of mathematics teaching, while containing many practical ideas and suggestions for structuring teaching and encouraging learning. It contributes to the expectation that:

> *Throughout their careers, teachers will continue to improve their teaching skills, and keep up to date with the subject and its pedagogy, so that they can teach mathematics rigorously and in a way which communicates their enthusiasm for the subject to pupils, in order to stimulate pupils' intellectual curiosity and to maintain and raise standards of attainment.* (Teacher Training Agency, 1998, p. 4)

RESEARCH IN MATHEMATICS EDUCATION

The approaches in this book are all supported by research, but we have decided not to give references throughout the book except where we feel the reader might like to know about our sources and inspirations for mathematics teaching and learning. The text seemed to be complex enough without being interrupted by references. This may leave us open to the charge of being highly opinionated and subjective in some of our assertions, but we do include brief bibliographies intended to account for our assertions.

However, teaching is necessarily framed by beliefs. Teachers have beliefs about how students learn in general, how they learn mathematics in particular, what mathematics is, what it means to know and understand mathematics and how much can be known about someone else's mathematical knowledge. In all of these areas there is much disagreement in the research community and among theoreticians. In the light of these conflicts it is important to indicate at the beginning what our beliefs are.

BELIEFS ABOUT MATHEMATICS

Traditional approaches to mathematics teaching have assumed that mathematics is a system of structures which people have to uncover and come to understand. It has been seen as a pure form of thought and the appropriate model for all thinking. Currently it is more usual to see it as having been created by mathematicians in response to a variety of needs and interests, and consisting of conventional symbols and relations which have commonly accepted meanings. Its relationship to logical thought, numeracy and high-technological work gives it great importance in the school curriculum. The knowledge that mathematics is created by human thought, and discussed and refined over time by people who use it or study it, indicates that 'doing' and 'thinking' mathematics are more important aspects to develop than performance of techniques and knowledge of facts, particularly now that much can be done by hand-held technology. Nevertheless, the ability to use and apply the techniques and facts of mathematics is important because they can be used to explore more complex mathematics and they might be useful in other areas of activity. Sometimes mechanical knowledge, such as rote-learnt methods, can lead to insight about meanings and understandings. For example, knowing the rhythms of the eleven-times table can help students become curious about its structure, and can offer a way to learn more about place value when the rhythm breaks down for larger numbers. Mathematics, while having a formal conventional symbolism and structure, can be discussed in everyday language while those who work with it test its characteristics, properties and limitations.

BELIEFS ABOUT HOW STUDENTS LEARN MATHEMATICS

Students develop their own ideas of the structures of mathematics. The more this construction is encouraged and guided by exploration, interaction and discussion, the more the students' ideas will fit together to form a coherent network. The facts and techniques which are necessary to fit into an understood network and are hence easier to recall, adapt and use.

Doing mathematics requires some very fundamental characteristics of human thinking. Students have to be able to decide when something is generally the case, or only sometimes the case. This is a basic part of learning language and of reasoning in other areas of human endeavour, so it can be safely assumed that students have this ability. They also have to be able to understand number as a characteristic of groups of things, an ability which exists in very young children. They have to be able to see when things are the same and when different, again a fundamental linguistic ability. They have to be able to understand combinations of simple elements of mathematical communication. All these powers can be used and developed in the mathematics classroom.

It is commonly believed now that all learning involves the learner interacting with the environment through experience and making sense of those experiences personally and through communicating with others. The model of teaching and learning that suggests that the teacher can somehow transfer knowledge into the student's head is less useful than models that depend on interaction because it does not explain how some students are able to learn mathematics by listening to explanations and copying examples whereas others cannot. Teachers who are aware that students are making their own sense of mathematics, whatever the lesson is like, are more likely to take student responses into account in their teaching, and to view them as tentative conjectures rather than as right or wrong answers. In our teaching, we developed classrooms in which conjecture, exploration, holistic tasks, variety of approaches to learning, discussion and argument were commonplace features. Within this environment, the mathematical meanings constructed and discussed were more likely to be seen as part of a whole complex structure, rather than as isolated topics which require apparently meaningless manipulation of symbols. Students were more likely to see connections between the mathematics they did in school and that which they met outside school.

BELIEFS ABOUT MATHEMATICAL ABILITIES

The propensity to generalize, to discriminate, to ennumerate, to appreciate spatial properties and to complexify arguments might be an innate feature of human minds, but we are not saying that mathematical abilities are themselves innate and fixed. Rather, we would suggest that mathematical abilities can be developed in response to experiences and environments, including being taught. However, there has been a tendency to assume that students are pre-programmed to have different levels of mathematical achievement. The notion of a fixed ability is sometimes evidenced when students are placed into sets or curriculum tracks which limit what they are offered, when teachers 'deliver' a curriculum in a predetermined way without adapting it to students' responses, when testing is only of one type designed to show a mechanistic construction of the subject, and when teachers predict examination outcomes several years ahead of the examination.

In countries where educating everyone to a certain basic standard is more important than educating selected individuals to be high achievers, mathematics standards, according to international tests, appear to be higher. Videos of classrooms in Pacific Rim countries do not show mechanistic, formalistic teaching but instead show shared problem-solving, discussion and argument. Students observed in mixed-ability Russian and Hungarian classrooms work on mathematics at a much higher level than their contemporaries in UK and USA. Mathematics, as an intellectual activity rather than a desired qualification or an aid to employment, has a higher status among educated people in some countries than in others. We could go on, but the point we are trying to make is that the assumption that students have fixed abilities which limit their potential achievement in mathematics is not universally held. The expectations of society and the education system have a major part to play in establishing expectations.

What are your beliefs about mathematics, how students learn mathematics, and mathematical activities?

Given that a mathematics qualification is an important passport to higher education and further social and economic opportunity, it is especially important that mathematics teachers do not limit the possibilities for their students.

Some common features of teachers whose work we admire are: reluctance to accept that some students might be unable to learn mathematics; acceptance of the responsibility to find ways to help them learn; willingness to work on the structures of mathematics to devise tasks which recognize and use structure and connection; recognition and exploitation of students' ways of thinking. This book is about the ways in which we, and others, try to carry out these tasks and we include ourselves as open to criticism for often failing to include these features in our teaching. It is also about a view of what is worthwhile in mathematics as a human endeavour, and helping students find out what is worthwhile for themselves.

NOTE

1. See, for example, Boaler (1997), Low Attainers in Mathematics Project (1989)

REFERENCES

The Association of Teachers of Mathematics can be found at: www.atm.org.uk

Boaler, J. (1997) *Experiencing School Mathematics*. Buckingham: Open University Press. This book describes a study of two schools with similar intakes. In one school mathematics was taught in mixed-ability groups, using an activity-based approach; in the other students were taught in 'ability' groups and traditional styles were used. National examination results in the first school were better than those in the second.

Low Attainers in Mathematics Project (1989) *Better Mathematics*. London: HMSO. This book records the results of a study in improving mathematics teaching for low attainers. The authors found that such students responded well to challenges and exploration, in contrast to the usual view that they should be given simplified, step-by-step work.

Qualifications and Curriculum Authority (1999) *Mathematics: The National Curriculum for England*. London: Department for Education and Employment.

Teacher Training Agency (1998) *Initial Teacher Training National Curriculum for Secondary Mathematics* (Annex G of circular 4.98). London: Department for Education and Employment.

Part One
Teaching for Inclusion

—2—
Atmosphere and culture

If your closest friends were to walk unexpectedly into your classroom, what would you want them to see and hear? Would you wish these sights and sounds to be any different if a professional colleague were to walk in?

You might have an instant single answer to these questions, or you might prefer to describe different features depending on your aims and intentions for different lessons.

If we asked you to describe a 'best' lesson what would you offer? What images come to mind? Would this lesson be the same if you were being inspected?

Thinking back to your own school days, what were the most memorable lessons you attended? Whom did you regard as your best teachers?

Comparing the features you have selected to answer these questions might show a similarity of values, or might show differences. Sometimes unusual teachers have more impact than their orthodox colleagues.

If you have children who are currently passing through the school education system, what kind of lessons would you wish them to experience? What qualities would you want their teachers to exhibit?

When we talk of classroom culture we are referring to the collection of habits, rules, expectations, actions, interactions, beliefs and values which you and your students establish and understand. When we talk of atmosphere we refer to the manifestations of culture in individual lessons, or in moments in the lesson. For instance, you may be working to establish a culture of independent learning; the atmosphere which your visitor may perceive is one of students doing a variety of different things, using different books and resources, grouping themselves in a variety of ways.

To describe the culture of your classroom it might be helpful to list typical elements which constitute your classroom atmosphere. Your list may differ from ours in focus, as well as in what you describe. Our list is set out in three sections: student actions and behaviour; teacher actions and behaviour; and classroom environment.

In writing this list we recognize we give an idealized and selective picture of our classrooms. The reality is that they are unpredictable places, changeable according to a whole host of factors over which the teacher may have little or no control (such as the weather, the time of day, the previous lesson, the content of the previous nights' popular TV programme). They are filled with dynamic beings, charged by emotions and relationships. Furthermore, classrooms have enormous pressures placed upon them by parents, religions, politicians, inspectors, the media, colleagues, ourselves and, of course, the students. Nevertheless, underlying coherence is achieved through the classroom culture; students and teacher still know roughly what to expect from each other.

ELEMENTS OF THE AUTHORS' CLASSROOM CULTURE

In terms of student actions and behaviour we would like students to: engage purposefully in their mathematical work; ask questions of each other; ask questions of the teacher; ask for help; offer help; take independent responsibility for their work; respect each others' right to work and ways of working.

As teachers we expected to: have a working relationship with students; respond seriously to, as well as initiate, interactions; prepare interesting approaches to mathematics; ensure students have access to appropriate mathematics; use a range of resources, teaching styles and strategies.

As for the classroom environment, we expect it to: be sometimes calm and at other times vibrant, but always purposeful; be used flexibly with people, desks and chairs rearranged to suit the mathematical activities; contain a variety of easily accessible resources; have displays produced by students, teachers and publishers.

Giving meaning to these lists is highly subjective. For instance, one definition of *working relationships* will differ from another. It is important to reflect upon the nature of the working relationships one wishes to achieve before determining how one might set out to achieve them. A fundamental tension we experienced in our teaching was how the desire to allow independent directions of study conflicted with the desire to give all students access to the mathematics on the syllabus; how far should the teacher force students to work in certain ways or on certain topics? Another tension was between the desire to establish a respectful working relationship and the need to establish helpful modes of behaviour in the early stages of working with a class; how can a teacher do this without being authoritarian at first? Teachers' actions and behaviour are dealt with in other chapters of this book, and can also be found in the passages that follow because, in many cases, students' behaviour can be influenced by the model the teacher generates of being both a mathematician and a supporter of learning.

STUDENTS' ACTIONS AND BEHAVIOUR

Students engage purposefully in their work

It is too simplistic to contrast an over-zealous interpretation of purposeful engagement, where all students are made to behave as if working throughout a lesson, with an approach where students are entirely responsible for making decisions about when and how much work they do. The idea that purposeful engagement can always be identified by seeing students writing rather than apparently doing nothing is also naive. In practice it is necessary to seek a balance between concentrated mathematical activity and more relaxed, reflective, approaches to work. Mixtures of practical and mental activity, or the interspersion of exploration and recording, provide useful contrasts.

One way of ensuring such mixes, and hence recognizing the need for variety in studious activity, is to help students develop attitudes of personal responsibility for their learning. Here again we might find a tension between the teacher's desire for students to behave autonomously and the need for students to be persuaded to pursue certain possibilities, and to be convinced that they are worthwhile. For students to take personal responsibility, opportunities and encouragement must exist for them to make decisions about the direction, amount, pace and depth of work they do. There are implications here for short-term lesson planning, long-term curriculum planning, the resources and the strategies used. Ever-present is the issue of when the teacher can 'let go' and when to be more assertive.

How, then, is the teacher to exercise the obvious responsibility for 'coverage' of the examination syllabus? Firstly, students can only make responsible decisions if they are fully aware of what they need to do for examinations and other assessments. The syllabus and assessment criteria have to be shared with the students so they are not fully dependent on the teacher for monitoring progress and suggesting suitable directions of study. Secondly, the teacher must provide adequate opportunities for all students to work on syllabus topics. Thirdly, if students are used to developing their own deep understandings of mathematics in various contexts, the inclusion of extra topics specifically for examination purposes is easier, because they are being incorporated into a constructed network of meanings, rather than learnt as extra, unconnected algorithms. For example, students who are used to finding their own ways of learning and using technical terms, and have worked on ratios to their own satisfaction in a range of contexts, are likely to find it easier to learn how to use trigonometric ratios than those for whom topics have been presented as given techniques to be used in a defined range of questions.

One manifestation of the classroom cultures outlined above is a reluctance to use exclusion or detention; our belief is that these can be counterproductive to the aim of independence, particularly if they operate in a solely punitive way. What should be done if students choose an inappropriate course of action? One of the main challenges for teachers is to find ways of dealing with low-level disturbance caused by some students chattering about other topics. Another is to motivate those who find it difficult to operate in the classroom. We do not claim to be able to keep all students productively involved with mathematics all the time; nor do we equate 'productive work' with 'writing' or 'working through a textbook'. We *do* claim, based on our own experience in schools, some of which served areas of social deprivation and dysfunction, that students who are expected, and trusted, and given the knowledge and tools to behave responsibly will do so, by and large.

In reality our classrooms displayed a balance of authority and control, with responsibility constantly shifting between the teacher and the students.

For students to engage purposefully with their work they must see what purpose their work has in the first place. This might involve creating opportunities to tackle questions like, 'What is the point of learning mathematics?' This can be a challenge to teachers who have not considered, for some time, why they are teaching mathematics. Offering responses such as: 'Well, when you get a job . . .' or 'So that you know where to stand when the tree falls down . . .' or 'Because it's on the exam . . .', do not convince children of the real value of mathematics and indeed are often false. In everyday and work situations school mathematics is rarely used. If the purpose is merely to pass examinations, then training in examination questions might be a more effective way to teach than approaches based on developing mathematical understanding. Therefore, we believe it is important to be explicit with the students about the values of learning mathematics.

What are your perceptions of the values of learning mathematics?

How do you communicate these to all your students?

How do you help students understand and believe, for themselves, these values?

One strategy that we have used, often at the beginning of a new school year, is to push the desks to the edges of the room, put all the chairs in a ring, then, once everyone is present, ask them, 'Why do *you* think it is important to learn mathematics?' Another approach is to ask students regularly to consider what they have learnt in a particular sequence of lessons.

Not much secondary mathematics is of direct use as a tool, without adaptation, in contexts other than more complex mathematics. The purposeful atmosphere in our classrooms was generated by the inherent intrigue of the mathematics itself, rather than its potential uses. Puzzle-like aspects of it engendered delight by showing similarities in unexpected places. Often this was achieved through solution of a problem. Sometimes, but not always, pleasure was gained from getting a correct answer, playing games, making decisions, exploring ideas, investigating the best way of doing something, choosing the best course of action; these are the kinds of activities that we deal with many times each day in and out of school. Mathematics provides us with the mental tools to solve some of these types of problems, ways of thinking which help us tackle new kinds of problem, and mathematizing abilities which can be used to transform problems into solvable forms. Jo Boaler, comparing students' mathematics in two very different teaching environments (1997) showed that students who are encouraged to work in these ways, led by thinking processes rather than by content, do indeed make a connection between the ways of working in the mathematics classroom and mathematizing problems in the outside world.

The challenge is to find problems and puzzles that develop the use of thinking skills and the understanding of mathematical concepts. Activities often described as investigations, involving creation of data sets from patterning situations and expressing them in general terms as formulae, do not always offer obvious opportunities to work further on the concepts usually taught in secondary mathematics. However, the *processes* used in such activities can be employed in working towards conceptual understanding of mathematics. Working from examples and manifestations of concepts, describing similarities and differences, articulating common features, deriving formulae and properties from such common features, using different representations, applying concepts in slightly different formulations are all processes which can enhance learning. Such approaches pose challenges, capture interest and imagination and tap into natural curiosity and creativity.

Students ask questions of each other, of the teacher and readily ask for help

There are many different types of questions that students might ask. There are service questions such as, 'May I borrow a pencil?'; requests for help such as, 'I don't understand, please can you help me?'; those which seek confirmation and affirmation such as, 'Is this the right answer?'; and more challenging questions such as, 'Why are we doing this?'

Responses, even to the first type, are conditioned by the classroom culture. A classroom in which students can borrow pencils as they perceive the need has a different atmosphere from one where such a question is the trigger for a lecture about coming to class properly prepared. Responses to all these types of question can be chosen to encourage the development of independent working practices, thoughtful approaches to education, personal choice, classroom discussion and to raise students' awareness of their own learning.

We would go far beyond this and suggest that appropriate questioning could be at the heart of learning mathematics. When students ask questions we can tap into their natural inquisitiveness. We can show them how questions such as: 'What if ...?' 'How many ...?' 'Have I found them all?' 'What else could happen?' reveal ways to explore concepts, topics and ideas. Students can be encouraged to ask questions through routines in which the class shares a variety of questions that occur to them about a mathematical situation or problem. It can become a feature of classroom life that students are expected to pose questions before they begin to answer any. Particular forms of question can enter into the accepted habits of the classroom, becoming elements of the culture. For example, the question 'are there any counter-examples?' is used frequently in the development of new mathematical ideas, and also enables students to explore the meaning of a new (to them) concept. A teacher can work deliberately towards getting students to use it regularly in a variety of situations (see Chapter 4).

To engender a questioning culture it is necessary to demonstrate explicitly that questioning is healthy, valuable and desirable, and also to demonstrate different forms of question which the teacher, as the expert mathematician, knows to be useful for advancing mathematical knowledge and understanding. However, this has implications for the types of learning experience and the nature of the tasks and problems posed by the teacher in the first place. It suggests a scheme of work based on a question-centred, problem-posing and problem-solving pedagogy.

If questioning is encouraged at all levels in the classroom, this challenges the stereotypical view that teaching mathematics involves the teacher asking the students a number of closed, rhetorical questions, to which they are expected to provide specific answers. A teacher has to be aware that students who have been used to the latter approach might well take time to adapt to a different kind of classroom dynamic. Once habitual questioning between students, as well as between students and teachers, is achieved it is less likely that a student who has misunderstood something would allow much time to pass without seeking assistance. But there is a balance of responsibility between the teacher and student; the teacher may need to accept that a student may feel intimidated, or foolish for not knowing what to do, even if the accepted classroom practice is to ask freely for help. Alternatively, the student might not be interested in the work or may have other pressing issues of adolescence in mind. The teacher might wonder if hidden aspects of the school culture (such as bullying) have contributed to the situation. The ways students respond will depend not only upon the quality of relationships with their teacher but also on other relationships and pressures, in and out of the classroom.

Students offer each other help

The use made of different students' strengths and the value given to mutual help are central aspects of classroom culture. If the teacher starts every new topic as if no one has any prior knowledge or useful insights, and students are always in the role of consuming or receiving what the teacher offers, then independent working and questioning would be impossible to achieve. Once a student has an understanding of a concept or demonstrates an expertise to perform a certain skill (such as rounding a value to a number of decimal places), there exists the possibility of the student acting, briefly, as another teacher in the classroom. This expertise can be called upon whenever needed. What has to be avoided is the syndrome of some students always being expected to help others, when they could be exploring more mathematics of their own, and others only rarely offering help.

Where students carry out teaching roles there is a three-fold benefit. The first is to shift authority, temporarily, to students. The second is that students who offer help will deepen their knowledge of the concept. Thirdly, during such interactions there exists more than one teacher in the classroom, and hence more than one way of teaching. Explaining to students the type of help they might offer and that to give an answer might not be the most profitable form of help, is an important aspect of this strategy.

Students take independent responsibility for their work

A strange event seems to take place for many students between the last term of primary and the first term of secondary school. This is an apparent loss of independence and personal responsibility. Whenever we visit primary schools we are struck by the impression that students are developing important skills of self-reliance and autonomy. Yet, when the same students arrive in a new school they appear to exhibit a new helplessness. This is understandable; they are new small people in a large school, where there are new rules, norms and fears. Typical questions such as: 'Shall I underline the date?' 'Shall I use a ruler?' appear to symbolize this loss of confidence, but are more likely to be an expression of a desire not to get things wrong in this new place, with new teachers. It is tempting for secondary teachers to assume that students cannot take responsibility for themselves. However, in most cases it can be assumed that students can act responsibly, but need to be given encouragement, permission, and structures within which to do this. Again the culture of the classroom is crucial, manifested in the multi-faceted, many-layered, moment-by-moment events that students sense and interpret; these help determine how much personal responsibility individuals will learn to take. Setting the scene for students to exercise their sense of responsibility within a problem-posing, problem-solving classroom culture can start in the first moments of mathematics in a new school.

A key factor in shifting responsibility to students is the number of opportunities to make decisions about the direction and quality of work they do, and with whom they choose to work.

Students respect each other's right to work and ways of working

A teacher who respects all students' ways of working, where they are not preventing others from working, can model listening and questioning as acceptable ways to respond to different views and methods. The way a teacher deals with completely wrong answers, confusions, misunderstandings and so on can set the tone for how students react to each other's ideas.

THE CLASSROOM ENVIRONMENT

Some teachers are fortunate to have a room in which they do most or all of their teaching. Under such circumstances, opportunities exist to make the room a place which expresses the teacher's values. Mathematics departments without dedicated subject rooms are seriously disadvantaged in not being able to create essentially mathematical environments. Those departments which have dedicated rooms are in a strong position to create an environment with displays, posters, artefacts and prevailing conversation which supports the atmosphere of inclusion, enquiry and discussion.

Calm and vibrant, purposeful classrooms

Rather than having a fixed view of what a purposeful classroom is like we suggest that the demands of the learning tasks force certain kinds of atmosphere at different times. For instance, if students are exploring area by cutting and rearranging triangles to become trapezia, we would visualize a vibrant classroom with plenty of discussion and movement. A lesson in which students are monitoring their own understanding by working through written questions set by each other might be quieter, with students seated and silent, with some discussion or questioning of individuals at the end. It is not the case that a classroom has to be instantly comprehensible to a hypothetical visitor. It has to be comprehensible to the students and teacher in the context of the mathematical activity. It is as much a nonsense to have a silent practical lesson, with students forbidden to move without permission, as it is to have a noisy lesson when students are trying to construct reflective descriptions of their knowledge of a topic.

Resources and display work

What resources are always available in your classroom?

Freedom to choose approaches to mathematical tasks demands that appropriate resources are available for unexpected requests in every classroom. Resourcing is thus a manifestation of classroom culture as well as part of its creation. We write more about this in Chapter 6. The main issue here is that different resources are available and students are able to choose what to use without negotiation with the teacher. The teacher then acts as a questioner ('Why use X instead of Y?') rather than a custodian.

What is currently displayed on the walls of your classroom?
Why is it there and when is it used?

Display work is an important part of the environment, but it can be discouraging to see displays being damaged by a few students. It is worth maintaining high quality displays of students' work through regular repair with staplers, glue sticks and coloured masking fluids. The teacher can be more persistent in repair than students in doing damage.

What is the value of using class time to produce special display work? On one level, display work obviously enhances the classroom appearance. How much of the display is students' work, or photographs or published materials, will depend upon the intended use the teacher wishes to make of it and how frequently new work replaces old.

If, for example, the students are exploring the graphs of quadratic functions, one strategy is to ask each student, or pair of students, to produce a graph of the form $y = ax^2 + b$, where a and b take the values $\pm \{1/2, 1 \text{ or } 2\}$. Each graph is drawn on a prepared grid preprinted with the graph $y = x^2$, thereby enabling comparisons to be made. This task can be done in the last ten minutes of a lesson. Before the next lesson the teacher can mount all the labelled graphs on posters. The display becomes a focus for discussion in which students are asked to analyse the similarities and differences of the graphs produced. This strategy could also be used to explore graphs of linear or trigonometric functions. In this way students' work becomes a central learning resource.

Giving students the task of producing a poster to summarize the main aspects of their recent learning enables reflection and revision. Students might also be asked to consider a particular audience for their work, such as a younger class or a parent. Suggesting students write for an audience is a valuable strategy in a variety of learning contexts.

Another approach is to give students some brightly coloured sheets of A4 paper and, possibly for homework, ask them to make a poster to describe something they have understood about the current topic for revision purposes, or to describe their understanding of certain mathematical vocabulary. This approach can be used to record recent achievements or new understandings. For example, if students have just understood the process of rounding a figure to two decimal places, then they could be asked to make a poster which explains how this process is done.

Some teachers have a board for displaying work in progress, thus valuing rough, exploratory work and providing a forum for sharing current ideas. We know of one teacher who surrounds the classroom with all her students' project work, protected in plastic wallets and hanging by strings from pegs. Many teachers produce banks of interactive display materials and use them when appropriate for the current topic. Such displays can be models for questioning and problem-posing, and might even be starting points for new activities.

Posters and artefacts produced by publishers add colour and stimulation to a room, but are ignored if they become faded, tattered, and are not referred to during lessons.

Care and purpose can be demonstrated through the decisions the teacher makes about the classroom environment. If decisions are always made in ways which enhance the learning and teaching of mathematics, and are maintained with care, a purposeful learning environment can be more easily nurtured than in a temporary environment in which resourcing, arranging and displaying is accidental and hence incidental.

SUMMARY

In this chapter we have considered classroom atmosphere in terms of supporting independent learning, forming respectful relationships, helping students take responsibility for developing mathematical thinking and seeing links across areas of the mathematics curriculum. We wrote about students mutually supporting each other and being encouraged to question the purposes of learning mathematics. Using a problem-solving and puzzling approach to nurture students' inquisitiveness about the intrigue of mathematics enhances a questioning culture. We have also described the importance of the physical environment of classrooms, and considered the implications for resourcing and display work.

We have not dealt completely with every possible manifestation of culture, nor with every possible feature which conveys atmosphere to a visitor, but have given a range of issues and ideas which can be considered and incorporated into practice. The question we ask for every aspect of classroom atmosphere creation is:

How can you convey to students, through the classroom atmosphere, your beliefs about mathematics, encouragement for all to learn mathematics, and the ways of working that you value? What do your current practices convey to students?

REFERENCES

The book by Jo Boaler listed at the end of Chapter 1 relates to some of the ideas in this chapter also. Here are three references which describe how different beliefs lead to differences in teaching and testing styles, expectations and norms:

Lerman, S. (1990) 'Alternative perspectives of the nature of mathematics and their influence on the teaching of mathematics'. *British Educational Research Journal*, **16**, 15–61.
Nickson, M. (1992) 'The culture of the mathematics classroom: an unknown quantity?', in D. A. Grouws (ed.) *Handbook of Research on Mathematics Teaching and Learning*. New York: Macmillan.
Watson, A. (1999) 'Paradigmatic conflicts in informal mathematics assessment as sources of social inequity'. *Educational Review*, **51**(2), 105–15.

3

The dynamics of working with adolescents in the mathematics classroom

ADOLESCENTS AND SCHOOL

Adolescents learn to swear, smoke, drink, tell jokes; they learn the difference between 'indie' or 'techno' music; they learn how to walk with the right swagger, use fashionable language and choose clothes. They learn all this from each other, or from television and magazines, checked out with each other, often without asking or being told anything. They learn it very well, with no apparent effort, and incorporate many detailed discriminations into their knowledge. Being adolescent seems to have many of the features of apprenticeship models of learning, in which novices learn by watching experts, except that the 'experts' have only been adolescents slightly longer than the apprentices. Learning such complex social practices and subtle knowledge takes place within environments in which no overt teaching takes place, and in which the learners have high motivation to learn, and thus become part of the group. They are fulfilling a basic human need to be affiliated to a group.

Adolescents prove to us, through this behaviour, that they are capable of learning from conversation and imitation and through artefacts that can be obviously interpreted, such as music magazines, television programmes and advertisements, fashion objects, shared use of new technologies and so on. Talk is often used to make social statements, to convey status within a group, to test out ideas and ways of self-expression, and to show membership. Learning takes place by being involved with the group and its actions.

School is a place where adolescents come together in large numbers, and the social and grouping possibilities are multitudinous. Developing self-image and affiliation through interaction with others becomes a primary feature of school life; teachers might say that it detracts from schooling, but is it more likely that schooling, in the eyes of the adolescent, detracts from the rest of life?

For those who are used to interacting with only a few friends a room of thirty can be daunting. Being allowed or forced to sit in certain positions in relation to others in a classroom, three or four times a week, sets up its own possibilities for learning to be an adolescent, destructively or constructively. Students may be unable to avoid people they would not normally stay near; they may be unable to draw strength and identity from those they normally mix with. In addition, they have to maintain the language and social patterns on which they rely for status and affiliation; this may be in conflict with the languages and behaviour patterns they need to retain status and affiliation with the teacher, or the group as a whole.

Imagine one of your classes coming into the room to do mathematics; pick out the tenth student to enter and try to imagine what is going on in her head at that moment. How might you structure the start of the lesson to take account of her state of mind?

These potential sources of conflict are true in all schools. We do not intend, in this book, to discuss in general school policies or the pastoral role of teachers in this respect. Instead we will confine ourselves to teaching mathematics to these motley groups.

There are also other factors which indicate heterogeneity in all teaching groups. There may be differences in learning style, in relative strengths and weaknesses, in particular learning difficulties, in prior experience of ways of working, in mathematical knowledge and in self-image as mathematicians. These factors of adolescence suggest that all teaching groups are heterogeneous. However, the criteria used to create teaching groups in schools may have gone some way towards homogenizing certain groups. For instance, Walkerdine (1984) claims that to be seen as a good student one has to conform to expected norms of behaviour, and fit the teacher's image of 'a good student'. We could expect, therefore, students in a 'top' group for mathematics to be more homogeneous in some respects than those in a 'bottom' group who may not fit any of the other available categories.

Choose two 'top' group students; consider in what ways are they similar and in what ways different? Now choose two students from weaker groups; in what ways are these students similar and different?

What characteristics do you find yourself focusing on?

What qualities do you believe are important in the construction of groups of students?

How significant do these qualities become when students are in very mixed groups?

If we aim to develop individuals as mathematicians, it is often the case that the modes of assessment to which they will eventually be subjected value some kinds of mathematical behaviour more than others. So the question of how to work with mixed groups is influenced not only by the answers to the questions above but also by the prevailing assessment system.

Is your aim, for teaching mathematics, to somehow make a mixed group of students behave in the same way mathematically?

Or is your aim to help individuals develop their understanding of mathematics relative to their characteristics or predispositions?

A further influence is the teacher's own mathematical viewpoint, and such viewpoints may vary as much as those of students. For example, a teacher on an in-service course was kindly but firmly ridiculed by her colleagues, and later by her own son, for writing down an algebraic representation directly from considering a three-dimensional pattern. What was expected of all participants was to create a table of values and deduce the algebraic relationships from the numbers, rather than from the spatial characteristics. However, she was not behaving unconventionally in mathematical terms, merely seeing some mathematics in a different way to others. In fact, she saw it in a more abstract, sophisticated way which was not recognized by those around her who appeared to have a more limited view of the subject. In classrooms there are students and teachers who can work easily with the abstract, and other students and teachers who need to develop tables of values as an aid to abstraction.

In this chapter, as in the rest of the book, we shall look at typical strategies for coping with mixed classes in terms of how they allow individual ways of learning to develop. Because the educational aims of different departments have to be taken into account we are not intending to be judgemental about the values of certain strategies.

TALKING IN CLASS

Working alone

A classical way to focus minds on mathematics and avoid or diminish social interactions is to ask students to work on their own, in silence. One of us had to go into a mathematics classroom to give an urgent message to one of our own children, aged twelve. The mathematics lesson was in a silent room, all the children sitting at individual desks, heads down, writing. When an apology was given for interrupting a test the teacher looked puzzled. Later the child reported, with some surprise: 'It wasn't a test. It's maths. We always do it like that.' There was an assumption that another mathematics teacher should have understood this way of working.

The teacher seemed to believe that mathematics is a private mental activity and that students should all interact privately with text to learn the subject, and eventually to do written silent tests of it. It appears that in this classroom homogeneity was expected in terms of learning style and behaviour. This response to differences, to ignore them and to aim at uniformity by controlling interaction and behaviour, suits very few adolescents. There are times when silent working on their own can give students an opportunity to consolidate their own view of a topic and to think by themselves for a while. Yet consistently to deny them the chance to discuss their ideas, even in a structured way, is to deny them a valuable way of construing mathematics.

Allowing talk

What do students talk about in your classes?

Different teachers allow pupils to talk in classrooms for a variety of reasons. Some teachers have said to us:

It helps them be more relaxed.

I am happy for them to socialize a bit so long as they get on with their work.

Adolescents like to talk and if you don't let them you just make trouble for yourself.

As well as these social reasons for allowing talk there are strong reasons for encouraging talk in the learning of mathematics. Lev Vygotsky, the Soviet psychologist who has influenced many educational thinkers to promote discussion in classrooms, believed thought and language to be intimately connected and develop concurrently in interactive social situations, such as the home, the playground or the classroom. Whether one agrees that thought can or cannot occur without language, it is generally agreed that talk is an important aid to learning. We have found David Pimm's ideas are useful here:

> *Within the educational context of a mathematics classroom there are two main reasons for pupils talking, namely talking to communicate with others and talking for themselves ... Talking for others, in an attempt to make someone else understand something or to pass on some piece of information, is one of the many communicative functions spoken language permits.*

> *Talking for themselves involves situations where pupils may be talking aloud, but where the main effect is . . . to help organise their own thoughts.*
> (1987, p.23)

But simply allowing talk is not enough in itself. Lee (1997), a teacher researching in her own classroom, tape-recorded discussions among her students. She comments that, during certain kinds of activity, there was plenty of talk but it turned out to be mainly unrelated to the mathematics. For instance, students were apparently able to work through programmed textbooks while talking about other matters. When asked what they were doing in mathematics, a typical reply might be, 'I'm on the red table and we do book 3'. During tasks which were practical or investigative the discussion was of entirely different kinds which she identified as: readings of the question; statements of the problem; statements about what they were going to do; observations and theories about mathematics; working out loud; challenging and answering observations and theories; and statements of uncertainty. She concluded that all students are able to engage with such discussion, so long as tasks allow, require and encourage it. Different learners contribute different perspectives to the work. Those who learn better in social interaction, and those who prefer silent interaction with a text, are both catered for and encouraged to experience each other's ways of working.

Mathematical discussion

Language has a wider role than the kinds of discussion described above. It is also valuable for developing an understanding of an abstract concept. This occurs through conversation, exposition, the written page, or muttering to yourself. The importance of private language and inner monologues cannot be overstated. Even the way we read mathematical symbols out loud can affect understanding. Compare, for example, the potential usefulness of reading $\frac{3}{4}$ as 'three-quarters' with reading it as 'three line four', as we heard from a student who had learnt mainly from textbooks. Mathematical words and descriptions are linked with symbols and meanings of some sort; finding symbols to convey the same meaning as words do is therefore fundamental to the development of mathematical thinking.

Encouraging reading mathematical text and paying attention to how it is read, whether it is the student's own or someone else's, can make mathematics easier to 'know'. For example, 'a half of a quarter' is easier to visualize, and hence calculate, than the symbols '$\frac{1}{2} \times \frac{1}{4}$'. Reading '20% of 32' aloud almost tells you how to calculate it. Saying '23×47' aloud encourages you to deal with the 'twenty' and the 'forty' separately rather than get bogged down in a written algorithm starting with the 7 and the 3.

These are relatively trivial examples; it is much more instructive to listen to students trying to explain their mathematics to one another and to ourselves. In that kind of situation you can sometimes hear real struggles to make sense of symbols and get underneath them to the structure of what is happening, as Lee observed. Teachers might then overhear some very challenging comments between students, such as: But what do you mean? But why have you done that? But where did this measurement come from?

Structuring talk

Try to bring to mind a time when you first taught a mathematical topic. As a result of trying to teach the topic, did you ever find that you 'properly' understood some of the concepts involved for the first time?

Teachers frequently report the experience of understanding a topic more deeply through teaching it. A typical statement is, 'I never really understood negative numbers (or calculus, or something else) until I had to teach it to someone.'

You will recognize this scenario; it gives a substantial reason for getting students to work together, talk about their work, explain it to each other and make meaning together. They may need to be taught or reminded how to do this. Discussion will have little or no value if one student gives an answer to a problem and the other student just writes it down, uncritically, right or wrong. When work is structured so that students *have* to talk with each other, or with teachers, about mathematics the quality of learning will be improved. Unfortunately there are some children who are brought up not to argue but to acquiesce, and certainly not to argue with their teachers. It is important, therefore, to provide students with opportunities to understand these different expectations, so that they can take part in and contribute to the different cultures in their classrooms, where 'arguing' mathematically with the teacher and each other is strongly encouraged.

One such method was described to us by a group of Russian mathematics teachers.

> **Ludmilla:** *They use worksheets. When a child has finished her work she raises a card with a green number. If a child needs help she raises a card with a red number and if the green and red numbers match they get together and talk and the child with the green number explains until the red number understands. If this doesn't work they both raise a blue number and I explain until they understand and they are given the next worksheet.*
> **Visitor:** *What is on the worksheets?*
> **Ludmilla:** *An explanation and some examples. I write them all myself.*

Tamara: *You should see it: all the talking and noise and cards waving . . . and Ludmilla running about. . . .*

If we do not allow talking in our classrooms our students can miss out on so much that could be stimulating. We have said that it is not enough just to 'allow' talking. Students may have to be helped to learn how to talk and argue about mathematics and need to have something to talk to each other *about* and this is less likely to occur if they are working on individual pathways. If, however, they are working on a shared task or the same activity, perhaps using some apparatus, or producing a poster or report of their work, then there is something to talk about. Clearly mathematical tasks which are intriguing, stimulating and grab students' attention are more likely to encourage such talk.

SEATING AND GROUPING

Seating as a disciplinary issue

When and why do you move students in your classes?

How often do you use different seating or furniture arrangements?

How often do you consider making changes to the grouping of students within classes?

At a basic level 'seating' could be about who sits next to whom. Seating is often used as a management tool to produce good discipline. New teachers are often advised to seat students alphabetically, or alternating boys and girls, or to split troublesome pairs and strategically place those who 'know how to behave' alongside those who find it hard to settle to work. Moving pupils from one place to another is often a disciplinary matter, pupils being allowed to stay where they are unless they cannot behave properly, in which case they may be moved to another place nearer to the teacher, or further away from trouble. How frequently are pupils moved for positive reasons to promote learning? We talk more about furniture arrangements in Chapter 6.

Seating as a learning issue

Who works best with whom in your classes?

What kinds of responses do you receive when you ask students to move?

Purposeful mathematical discussion requires that some attention be given to grouping within classrooms. Sometimes we might let students sit where and with whom they wish. Sometimes we have moved students for reasons we would define retrospectively, with some embarrassment, as disciplinary. We say 'embarrassment' because the classroom is a place for learning and self-discipline and, if we have taken individual needs into account, then we should not have to take action which is purely disciplinary. This may seem an unrealistic stance, but we present it as a belief, rather than something we always achieved!

One way to assist learning is to seat a weaker student next to a stronger student, whose job it then becomes to explain the mathematics to the weaker one. Although this promotes some of the virtues of mathematical talk, it can be a one-way conversation, and deprives the stronger student of stimulation by others. As such this can only be a transitory strategy, used alongside other strategies. Another common way is to group students within a classroom together according to perceived mathematical strengths, so that students are stimulated by dialogue with their intellectual peers. The disadvantage of this is to deprives weaker students of conversation with stronger ones. Furthermore this strategy will depend upon the teacher grouping appropriately. There is immense practical value in collecting a group of students together who, we recognize at that moment, are all working on a similar problem and offering them a common extension task to work on. We try to avoid keeping such groups fixed over time.

Using flexible seating arrangements

A flexible combination of ways, chosen according to the learning task, would maximize the advantages for all students and allow the teacher some flexibility in deciding who could best work with whom for the particular tasks, rather than making semi-permanent seating decisions. A further argument for flexibility is that groups who commonly work together create patterns of working that may be supportive and agreement-based rather than stimulating and challenging. Hence a change of groups can lead to new ways of working together and new insights into ways of thinking about mathematics. If flexibility and change become part of the culture of the classroom, students will expect to work with several different people, and new interests can be harnessed as they arise in the classroom. Two students, at opposite sides of the room, who approach a problem in *similar* ways can be asked to move to work together without resentment, thus prompting explanation and support. More interestingly, two students who have approached a problem in *contrasting* ways can be moved to work together, thus provoking discussion and a need for resolution.

One of us had a group of female students who always worked together producing identical, neat, rather uninspiring work. Their whole sense of confidence in mathematics and in school appeared to be based on membership of this group, but the effect on their study was a downward spiral in which nothing happened mathematically which was not with the full agreement of the group. The purpose of the group became agreement and safety instead of argument and risk and the outcome was the lowest common denominator of their possible achievement.

Being safe in a familiar group is not the same as developing confidence in mathematics. A further possibility created by a flexible approach to grouping is that a 'safety' group can be a home base but each member is expected, or even told, to work on her own or with someone new for parts of the work or for a certain time. One strategy can be to ask individuals to initially convince themselves of something, then convince a partner. This may be more likely to build real confidence in mathematical achievement. Perhaps students could start an activity together until they have some findings and then take those to another group to continue work. At the end of a piece of mathematics they can return to their preferred group and report on their work. In this way the group begins to function as a sounding-board and its members act as individual learners with personal contributions to make.

GROUP WORK

Structuring group learning

Work can be structured so that group work is essential to construction of meaning, for example:

- Structure a piece of work in such a way that two students each only have part of the story and have to discuss it to share ideas. An example would be to give half the class some numbers to square and add and give the other half the same numbers to use in the construction of right-angled triangles. They then have to collaborate to reveal Pythagoras' theorem.
- Structure a piece of work so that one student's information leads to one set of results and the other leads to an overlapping, but not identical set of results. They have to argue about what should, or should not, be included in the joint results. For example, one student could be asked to measure opposite angles of a range of quadrilaterals, another could be asked to measure opposite angles of a range of polygons inscribed in circles. Together they have the information which can lead to a generalization about the opposite angles of a cyclic quadrilateral.

- Give two students a plan and elevation of a complicated solid and ask them to describe it. Or give three pieces of information about triangles and ask students to use them produce at least two different triangles (if they can!)
- Ask pairs of students to sit back to back and for one to describe to the other, as over a 'telephone' a shape made from an agreed number of multi-link cubes, or a shape made on a nine-pin geoboard.
- Give some data about a controversial issue, for instance the volume of traffic on a ring road, and ask them to come up with arguments for and against adding an extra carriageway based on the data.

Pedagogic implications of group work

Some teachers consider grouping as an integral part of their planning for every lesson. For example, grouping can be for social purposes such as to integrate the class, or to enhance learning, to encourage discussion, to build confidence, or to allow collaboration over meanings and methods. Group work can also be used to involve students in sharing their existing knowledge and experience of a topic and thus learning from each other, particularly if they are working in an ethos which encourages critical listening. Sometimes working in groups helps students cut down some drudgery which may be involved in the work, like the generation of many different results or consideration of different cases. There is a tension here between using such work to provide plenty of practice through repetition, and maintaining pace and motivation by using a few, well-done, purposeful examples rather than many done mindlessly.

When teacher assessment and record-keeping was first introduced in the UK as a legal requirement, teachers were often concerned about how to assess the work students did while in groups. How could you know what was the contribution of one student or another? How could you be sure that an individual student had achieved anything at all other than copy the ideas and results of another? Of course, if assessment is seen as an attempt to produce a definitive statement of an individual's state of knowledge, assessing group work is problematic. Assessment of group work can be seen instead as an opportunity to assess informally the willingness and ability of a student to take part in mathematical conversations, contribute ideas, to pick up ideas from others, use them and express them in their own words. Such an assessment is necessarily subjective, so whether it should contribute in any way to formal assessment decisions is debatable. It is true that the teacher who is not with the group all the time cannot hear who has contributed what, but the finished product, be it separate written work, or a poster, or a verbal presentation, can show what has been learnt through the group's deliberations.

Like any other form of teaching, group work cannot be chosen merely for its social implications, nor rejected merely for difficulties over assessment. The prime question for teachers is 'In what circumstances does this method enhance the learning of mathematics?'

Whole class teaching

When do you expect students to work together as a whole group?

Is each student involved when you do this?

How do you structure work and discussion so that all students can make a real contribution to the mathematics?

Does the mathematics you use *need* the attention and contribution of the whole group; or do you choose to work with the whole group for reasons of economy and coverage?

For how long do you talk? For how long do you expect them to listen? How much will they hear? How much will they be able to retain?

It is sometimes enlightening to observe one's own behaviour when someone else is talking and you are expected to listen. Many reasonable adults find it difficult to concentrate for long without the urge to whisper, or allow their minds to wander and then return to find they have lost the thread or think, 'Why am I wasting time listening to stuff I don't need or don't understand?' Any or all of the students in front of you may be going through the same processes.

It may seem useful to restrict the use of whole class teaching to certain kinds of work, and keep the format of one person talking to a reasonable length. For example, whole class work can help to emphasize the value of listening to each other, or to introduce a new activity, or to run a discussion, or to orchestrate some kind of sharing of results or reporting back on work done. Whole class work can be deployed when playing games or doing physical activities, and to introduce and use mathematical terms and new concepts. Whole classes can explore ideas such as 'what is geometry?'. Whole classes can provide a forum for information about students' social context, such as having a discussion about personal budgeting to find out what aspects and values of money they are familiar with or interested in. Finally, whole group work is useful for some administrative purposes or when discussing acceptable ways of working.

In any group, even the most carefully selected, there will be students with a range of prior knowledge and motivations. It is tempting, therefore, to believe that only the briefest and most general of comments is likely to connect with all the students if you are talking about mathematical skills and techniques. For this reason, many teachers working with widely differing groups of students often use textbook or workcard schemes so students can work on different tasks. Consequently, the direct teaching is done by the text and not by the teacher. This pattern may be broken for occasional sessions such as work on number skills, or for practical or investigative work. We believe that this approach can exacerbate difference in mathematical achievement. The hard thinking of mathematics, the interaction with concepts, the development of personal understandings of mathematical structures, may only happen privately in one-to-one interaction with the teacher or, more often, with the textbook writer if there is little whole class teaching. But most students have few opportunities for one-to-one with the teacher in the average classroom. Dependence on textbooks assumes that students are skilled at grasping the intentions of the writers. Whole class teaching gives students access to the teacher's expert knowledge, the public use of mathematical language and ideas, and what other learners make of it.

In later chapters we describe many approaches to topics which can be used in order to involve the whole class in working on mathematical concepts, whatever the range of attainment so far.

SUMMARY

In this chapter we acknowledged that adolescents form their own views of the world and that they are quite capable of learning what they consider worth learning. We recognized the significance that identity, language, accepted social norms, status and relationships have upon patterns of behaviour and considered how it is possible to focus students' interest in mathematics.

Accepting the heterogeneous mix within all groups we questioned the feasibility of ascribing particular characteristics to 'high' or 'low' achieving groups. We described a range of whole class and small group teaching strategies and ways of organizing the classroom to help all students share knowledge in order to make sense of the language and symbols of mathematical concepts.

We completed the chapter by considering the limitations of textbook dominated learning and the impact of this upon whole class learning.

REFERENCES

Lave, J. (1988) *Cognition and Practice: Mind, Mathematics and Culture in*

Everyday Life. Cambridge: Cambridge University Press. Lave describes learning as essentially related to the social situation.

Lee, C. S. (1997) *Discussion in the Mathematics Classroom: Developing a Teacher's Awareness of the Issues and Characteristics*. Oxford: Oxford University Department of Educational Studies, Centre for Mathematics Education Research.

Pimm, D. (1987) *Speaking Mathematically: Communication in Mathematics Classrooms*. London: Routledge & Kegan Paul. A summary of the many aspects of language involved in teaching and learning mathematics.

Vygotsky, L. S. (1978) *Mind in Society: The Development of Higher Psychological Processes*. Cambridge, Mass.: Harvard University Press.

Walkerdine, V. (1984) 'Developmental psychology and the child-centred pedagogy: the insertion of Piaget into early education', In J. Henriques (ed.) *Changing the Subject: Psychology, Social Regulation and Subjectivity*. London: Methuen.

4

Mathematical interactions

In Chapter 2 we indicated some ways in which the teacher could, through interaction and other means, support the development of independent learning habits in the students. In this chapter we consider in more detail the kinds of interaction that teachers, support staff, parents and other adults might initiate in order to achieve this.[1]

In later chapters we show some simple ways to introduce potentially complex topics, so they can be accessed by nearly all students. Complexity can be built up by successive developments from a starting point.

The following sequence of questions illustrates an approach to coordinates, patterns of number pairs, graphs and linear functions:

I want you all to think about how you could mark four dots on a coordinate grid which would form a straight line.

If you have done that, how can you place four more dots to make a line parallel to the one you already have?

If you have done that, how can you describe the dots for a family of parallel lines on the grid?

Before we discuss these further you may like to consider some pedagogical issues:

How might you pose these questions: publicly to the whole class? privately to individuals or small groups? verbally or on a board or a display poster?

Can other supportive adults in your classroom pose these questions?

The teacher could then ask several students to give their responses to the first task. For example, some students may have confined their work to the positive quadrant, others to lines parallel to the axes, some may have a negative gradient, many will have spaced their dots at equal intervals, others may have varied the distances. All these ideas and results produced by students can be shared and made available for others in the class to use. One of the teacher's roles is to show students what is possible, and this can be achieved by showing that mathematics can be generated by themselves and their peers. Of course, if no one offers negative gradients or varied intervals, or any other less obvious solutions, teachers have to introduce these themselves.

The approach here is for the teacher to pose a simple task that can lead to a variety of responses; to anticipate some possible responses; to have a sense of developments of the topic and to cast these as extension tasks. There is enough challenge in this approach to keep a class of 15-year-olds thinking and learning and also enough to give all students the opportunity to contribute.[2] However, we do not expect students to 'discover' the mathematics involved; rather we intend them to have a range of experiences with a topic that can then be discussed. At a later stage, when there is already some understanding of the mathematics, formal notation and language can be introduced.

Another way to approach a topic simply, so all can be involved, is to invite a range of comments about a simple visual stimulus. For example, the teacher could ask for comments about a triangular piece of paper, a pair of numbers or a cuboid made from interlocking cubes. The aim is to capture the interest of many students rapidly, and to collect their perceptions, in order to relate what they see instinctively to the intended content of the lesson. This way of starting also signals possible alternative directions to the teacher. Further examples of ways to start working on mathematical topics can be found throughout the book, especially in the later chapters. In this chapter we focus on the quality of interactions during the lesson as part of the context for mathematical work, rather than on the starting tasks themselves. We start with a section on whole class teaching but most of what we say applies to whole group, small group *and* one-to-one interactions.

INTERACTION PATTERNS IN WHOLE CLASS TEACHING

The provision of suitable starting points is not enough on its own to ensure everyone participates. It is also important to manage whole class sessions so that all students have something to say, and are able to say it.

When you manage whole class discussions, what strategies do you use to involve all students in the interaction?

How do you involve them in thinking about the mathematics?

Who speaks, when and in what order?

Who does not speak?

One pattern of classroom interaction in mathematics is that the teacher asks closed questions. Some students raise their hands to respond. Their responses are given to the teacher, who approves or disapproves them; the pattern goes to and fro from the teacher to individual students. This interaction pattern is very common. Studies show that teachers typically wait a very short time for answers, so students who have to think quite hard may be left out of the system, recognizing that before they have answered one question the teacher will have speedily moved on to another. They may eventually give up trying to participate.

Sometimes this kind of interaction is called discussion. However, *real* discussion outside classrooms does not take this form but is more usually a to-and-fro between equals in which people can speak tentatively as well as with certainty. Somehow ways have to be found to encourage equal participation, listening and tentativity in mathematics classrooms.

Some teachers encourage wider participation by giving longer thinking time, asking students by name to answer, or asking everyone to write something on a piece of paper and hold it up so that only the teacher can see it. One technique is to forbid the raising of hands until everyone has had a chance to think, thus offering a response remains everyone's responsibility, and anyone could be asked to answer. Problems with this approach include possible boredom of those who have an answer straight away, and the risk that the person eventually asked is still unable to answer. However, if a question is open, with a variety of answers possible, and it is accepted in the classroom that answers can be partial or tentative, the latter problem is overcome. Also with open questions those who can quickly get an answer can be encouraged to think of more possibilities, or can be asked to generate answers which have specific properties.

Asking everyone to write three or four comments privately about what they can see in a situation, or what they already know, can be particularly powerful. Having done this the teacher can ask individuals for contributions and collect these on the board. Very quickly a lot of information can be gathered and discussed.

Another way to vary the pattern of teacher–student approval in whole class interaction, once it has been noticed, is by getting answers from several students and inviting others to agree or disagree with them; to elaborate on why they think an answer is correct; to explain how they think the student arrived at the answer; and to suggest methods by which the answer might be reached. In other words, the teacher can act as a springboard for ideas which are bounced to and fro between students, firstly with the teacher as coordinator and later as part of standard classroom practice.

A further variation is to hand responsibility over to the students for providing examples on which the lesson is based. The teacher provides the framework and shape of the lesson and the students provide much of the content. For example, in one lesson we watched, the teacher was constantly asking students to provide the raw material for the lesson. The following is an excerpt:

Teacher:	Actions:
Give me a number	Someone said 15
Give me a question, something with x in it, and x is 2, where the answer is 15	Someone gives an example
Everyone write down a question which has x in it and the answer is 15	The teacher selects two and writes them on the board like this:
	$7x + 1 = 15 \qquad 8x - 1 = 15$
What can I say about these two expressions?	Several respond that they are equal; the teacher calls them "equivalent"
So how can I write this?	A student writes $7x + 1 = 8x - 1$
Can I have a couple of diagrams to represent these then?	Students come to the board and draw representations of this equality

In all these strategies teachers remain in control of the social dynamics of the interaction. They can guide the direction of the discussion so that their curriculum intentions are pursued, and are open to students voicing their own ideas and understandings about the mathematics.

INTERACTIONS TO HELP STUDENTS DEVELOP THEIR THINKING

Teachers' interventions can provide further avenues of investigation while students are working. As well as the development of further questions as demonstrated above, teachers can, by the use of carefully chosen questions and prompts, guide students towards 'harder' mathematics, more complex ways of thinking, and in-depth exploration of their ideas.

Students learn how to think and talk about mathematics by hearing teachers and other adults doing so. Being in an atmosphere where thinking about mathematics is demonstrated frequently through the spoken word gives students models of useful ways to approach the subject, ways they might think about mathematics on their own or discuss it with other students. This involves more than imitation. There is wide agreement that learning takes place through interaction with experts who provide 'scaffolding' which shapes the way the learner shifts from one level of thinking to a higher level. In mathematics, scaffolding could consist of the use of questions and language forms which relate directly to mathematical thinking, such as: 'It looks as if . . .'; 'I wonder if . . .'; 'Is it sometimes true that . . .'; and 'is it not always true that . . .?'

These help students generate statements and conjectures which can then be explored, demonstrated or proved such as, 'It looks as if the gradient is zero at the minimum' and, 'I don't think it is always true that a series of decreasing terms converges'. A classroom in which these language forms are habitually used in public promotes good mathematical learning, for all students, in several ways. Such statements make public the tentativeness of mathematical thinking and promote confidence in raising questions, taking risks, verbalizing and discussing mathematics. In addition they provide models of language for imitation and frameworks for the learner to develop a personal inner speech of mathematical thinking. They are valuable tools to aid independent learning and study. In classes which consist of a small number of low-attaining students, it is very difficult to create and maintain such linguistically stimulating environments.

Some of these tools require the teacher to gradually withdraw as the expert, or only role model, handing responsibility over to students to take on these roles for themselves and each other. Independent learning in mathematics involves more than personal organization, planning, choice and evaluation skills; it also includes intellectual activity which relates to examining mathematical structures. A teacher may wish to encourage students to develop a habit of exploring properties because concepts emerge through identifying particular properties in mathematical situations. Three examples are:

A cylinder can be seen as a prism which has the particular property of a circular cross-section. Hence its volume can be seen to be conceptually related to the area of a circle.

The concept of congruency can emerge through matching common properties of shapes. Minimizing the number of common properties required for two shapes to be identical can lead to an awareness of conditions for congruence.

Describing the properties of a two shapes, one of which is the result of two reflections of the other, can develop knowledge of the relationships between rotations and reflections.

Exploring properties is both a way to understand mathematics, and to generate new mathematics. A classroom in which exploring properties is normal practice can encourage learners to do this habitually for themselves and hence become better mathematicians. Exploration of properties becomes normal behaviour if a teacher plans to include prompts to do so in her interactions both with individuals and with the whole group. It is particularly important to use a range of such interactions with the whole group so that students pick up the idea that this is common practice.

The following diagram summarizes the process by which the teacher helps the student become independent:

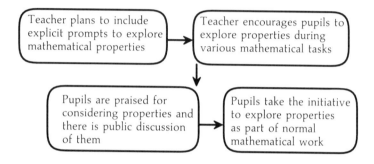

Fig. 1

The same process can be repeated for other mathematical activities such as 'verifying methods' or 'explaining connections'. In the next section we shall look at questioning as a way to promote more mathematical activity of this type.

MATHEMATICAL QUESTIONING

Make a list of questions you ask when you want to help students think further on their own.

When the teacher frequently uses similar prompts, students may come to realize that these are useful questions to ask. Well-known and much-used examples include: 'why ...?', 'what if ...?', and 'how can you be sure that ...?'

Most teachers have their favourite sorts of questions, designed to encourage students to think more deeply about the work they are doing, and these are most frequently used when students are working on investigative activities to show how they can use and apply mathematics. We wish to extend the range of such questions, and convince readers that they can be used throughout the teaching and learning of all mathematics, even the most procedural and algorithmic aspects. To do this we draw heavily on the much more extensive work on generic question types in Watson and Mason (1998).

Questions can be based on 'doing mathematics' as sequences of actions, rather than mathematics as various products, such as correct answers or finished written work. For example, students can be asked to think about 'proving' rather than produce proofs; to think about the process of 'calculating' rather than the answers; to think about 'equating' rather than solving equations. Another source of questions comes from looking at mathematical structures and guiding exploration of them. Better questions, in terms of developing mathematical thinking, come from asking what can be done next, rather than asking for factual answers.

Watson and Mason (1998) associate the following verbs with doing mathematics. It is not a complete list but illustrates the idea.

exemplify	organize	explain
specialize	change	justify
complete	vary	verify
delete	reverse	convince
correct	alter	refute
compare	generalize	conjecture
sort		

These verbs are applied to a list of the usual features of mathematics:

definitions	methods	justifications
facts	instructions	proofs
theorems	conjectures	reasoning
properties	problems	links
examples	representation	relationships
counterexample	notation	connections
techniques	explanations	

Suppose, for example, that percentages are to be taught. The teacher, while planning a lesson sequence, could choose almost any verb from the first list and any feature from the second to create a task for a class:

Correct this worked example
Explain the link between fractions and percentages
Give me an example of a way to represent percentages on a calculator
Change this problem about percentages so the answer is 42

Questions of this kind are more complex than following technical instructions, but provide rich material for whole class discussion, are necessarily open-ended, encourage students to think about concepts, rather than methods only, and develop their understanding. This structure for generating questions enables a teacher to construct mathematical challenges for standard curriculum content without recourse to textbooks. It also provides a framework for teachers to re-examine their own knowledge both at the planning stage and during classroom interactions.

It is also possible to generate mathematical challenges from published materials by applying the same kinds of questions to examples and exercises.

WORKING ON LANGUAGE

In any kind of classroom interactions, the teacher is the expert on mathematics and on useful language forms in which it is expressed. Students can hear the correct use of technical terms and practise using them in classroom interactions, but the importance of the teacher's language does not stop here. The teacher can also, through speech, emphasize important and de-emphasize unimportant features of the mathematical text. For example, when talking about adding fractions, a teacher can emphasize the numerators in '*three*-fifths add *one*-fifth equals *four*-fifths' in order to show how the numerators act as numbers of objects. Students are then encouraged to follow the same kind of emphasizing in their own mathematical utterances.

Reading questions out loud can help students understand what they are expected to do, and can reveal how much they understand of what is being said and expected of them. Both the teacher and other adults can ask students to read aloud and interpret what might be meant. The language of written questions, especially in tests, is very specific and can cause confusion. In the following example, a student who perfectly understood the situation mathematically answered incorrectly because she misunderstood the precision of the question:

How many tiles are needed for pattern number five?

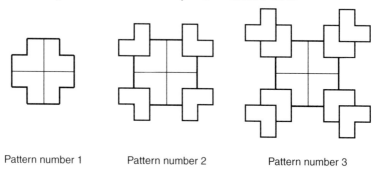

Pattern number 1   Pattern number 2   Pattern number 3

Fig. 2

She knew that eight more tiles were needed so she gave the answer '8'. She thought that, if she already had pattern number 3, she should ask for 8 tiles in order to make pattern number 5. She had been unable to discriminate between an ordinary request for '8 tiles' meaning '8 *more* tiles' and a mathematical request for 'a total of 20 tiles'. Hence, for her, the question was at best ambiguous, at worst, misleading.

As well as the teacher modelling and encouraging the use of technical language, the class might also learn: how to read and interpret written questions; the specific language of examination questions; what language patterns reveal about mathematics; how language can be used to develop understanding.

Another way to emphasize and de-emphasize particular features of mathematics is through careful and deliberate use of speech and silence. For example, in the following excerpt from a lesson, the teacher is getting the class to focus on particular aspects of constructing inverse functions.[3] The strategy is to offer students a simple problem, and, when it has been solved, getting students to say the numbers out loud and not say the operations:

Teacher:	Responses:
Think of a number, add 3, multiply by 4 and subtract 2. How can you get back to the number you started with?	The inverse function is eventually given as: 'add 2, divide by 4 and subtract 3'
So '. . . 3, . . . 4, . . . 2' becomes ?	'. . . 2, . . . 4, . . . 3'

Students are thus encouraged to emphasize the reversal of the numbers by being silent about the words. One could employ the same speech–silence strategy with the operations as the focus.[4]

REPETITION

Teachers often repeat what the students say to them in whole class situations. When what has been said is correct it is repeated it for emphasis and to make sure everyone has heard it. There may be other uses of repetition in the classroom, such as when students are asked to repeat something.

Does repetition by students have any value in the learning of mathematics?

This is in no way a plea for rote-learning. One recalls with horror children being forced to learn tables and humiliated if they did not manage to recite them. In many countries students are still expected to learn geometric theorems by heart when they, and some of their teachers, have little understanding of them. However, there may be language forms, technical terms, and ways of doing standard algorithms which, as part of a common culture, it is useful to repeat out loud to help them be remembered.

What mathematical sayings do you think it worth repeating out loud?

A powerful example of an imaginative use of chanting is given by Brown (1995). Learners are encouraged working rapidly in unison so that the sense of pattern and rhythm helps them work automatically, even intuitively, with number structures.

ANSWERING STUDENTS' QUESTIONS

Imagine a typical classroom situation in which students are working through exercises and occasionally putting their hands up to ask questions about what to do next, or what to do when they are stuck. What kinds of things do you say to them?

If we choose to work with individuals one-to-one, instead of stopping the whole class in order to clarify a particular point, there are several possibilities for response:

- giving a direct answer;
- showing what to do;
- getting the student to read the question out loud to see what sense is made;
- backtracking through previous questions to look for misunderstandings;
- getting the student to find useful features and patterns in previous questions;
- asking questions designed to take student through appropriate chains of reasoning.

A further possibility is 'funnelling' in which the student asks the teacher a sequence of questions which are successively more closely focused, leading the teacher eventually to do most of the reasoning and answer most of the questions!

If the teacher chooses to break out of the one-to-one interaction and to use the situation as an opportunity to offer other ways to work, there are further possibilities for response. A teacher can suggest working with another student for help or to struggle purposefully together. A classroom environment could be developed in which students ask each other questions before asking the teacher. A repertoire of mathematical strategies to use when stuck can be developed, such as: creating examples; working backwards from a possible answer; using a different way to represent the problem; developing self-questioning techniques that might be asked in such situations; recalling similar situations. All these strategies emphasize students' responsibility to do something rather than just give up, but more importantly offer the kinds of thinking they might usefully do now and in the future.

TELLING

Most of the questioning and interacting we have described above is initiated by the teacher. By modelling mathematical questioning the teacher can do much to encourage students to be questioning learners. Many times during the school day the teacher has to decipher what lies behind a question in order to decide how to answer it. We make in-the-moment decisions and have to differentiate between open types of question such as, 'What will happen if...?', indicating a preparedness in students to develop and extend their thinking, compared with more closed types of questions such as, 'Is this the right answer?', indicating a request for the teacher's confirmation. It can be frustrating for students to feel that all their questions are answered with questions or further challenges, but it can also be frustrating to be told an answer, or given a big hint, when you really want to work something out for yourself. What is important is for teachers to vary their responses. The dictum 'don't tell', which was a popular belief in the early 1980s, suggests that all mathematics can be rediscovered by students through exploration or reasoning. On the other hand, if the teacher always gives direct answers the student may never need to apply reasoning and conjecturing to mathematics.

How do you decide when and what to tell students?

Two stories illustrate how telling students a mathematical 'fact' can be useful, and need not stifle curiosity when students have already developed a questioning approach.

In the first incident, students were finding the largest box, in terms of capacity, which could be made from A4 card. They had been making cuboids, and had shifted to an abstract approach in which they calculated volumes of various hypothetical boxes. They wanted to consider cylindrical boxes, but did not know how to calculate the volume. They realized it would be 'area of cross-section times height'. The teacher told them the formula for area of a circle, and showed *pi* on a calculator. Her reason for telling them what they wanted to know was that they were in the middle of a complex mathematical task, in which they were highly motivated; all the 'understanding' they needed for this task was that the formula gave them the area! Later, when the whole class worked on circles, the students would come to understand more about it.

In the second incident, telling was more accidental. Katy and Jane were exploring recurring decimal sequences for sevenths. They had asked about the final '1' on their calculator display of 0.1428571 and the teacher told them it was the beginning of a recurring sequence. Katy and Jane were not satisfied with what they had been told and asked how they could know that the final '1' on their calculator was the first digit of a recurring sequence. The teacher showed them a long division algorithm in a mechanistic way. They went away and practised more long division sums involving sevenths, gaining an understanding of the process because they had a question for which the algorithm provided an answer. The 'telling' provided a starting point for further inquiry.

SUMMARY

We have explained strategies, interactions, questions and prompts to encourage student participation, to engage with mathematical thinking, during whole class discussions, in small groups and with individuals. We have described how different students might be encouraged to explore mathematical properties and structures.

We have examined the importance of language and how different teacher emphasis, including repetition and silence, can be used to promote understanding. We have offered a range of ways of asking questions to generate mathematical activity and conclude with a consideration of teachers telling or not telling students how to do something.

NOTES

1. In future any reference to 'other adults' includes support teachers, co-teachers, learning support assistants, parents, student teachers and any other classroom helpers.
2. This activity is especially challenging when done mentally, without paper!
3. Dave Hewitt, in a video produced for the Open University course EM235
4. A further use of silence is described in Chapter 6.

REFERENCES

Askew, M., Bliss, J. and Macrae, S. (1995) 'Scaffolding in mathematics, science and technology', in P. Murphy *et al.* (eds) *Subject Learning in the Primary Curriculum: Issues in English, Mathematics and Science.* London, Routledge. They discuss possibilities and limitations of classroom interactions within the complex demands of classrooms and education systems.

Brown, L. (1995) 'Shaping teaching to make space for learning', in *Mathematics Teaching,* 152.

Pirie, S. (1991) 'Peer discussion in the context of mathematical problem-solving', in Durkin, K. & Shire, B. (eds) *Language in Mathematical Education: Research and Practice.* Buckingham: Open University Press

Watson, A. and Mason, J. (1998) *Questions and Prompts for Mathematical Thinking.* Derby: Association of Teachers of Mathematics.

National Curriculum Council (1989) *Mathematics Non-Statutory Guidance: Section 3.0 Implications for planning and classroom practice* (London: HMSO) focuses on the difference between closed tasks (question) and modified tasks (open questions). It is now out of print but copies are in most schools.

—5—
Structuring the curriculum

In this chapter we consider the structure of the school mathematics curriculum, looking at teachers' responsibilities for planning schemes of work, individual lessons and sequences of lessons. In many schools teachers are expected to work with a given curriculum plan or scheme of work, so this chapter contains ideas for planning *within* a structure, as well as planning the structure itself.

Think about a recent topic you have taught: did you link it to other topics? Were you explicit about such links? Did you find ways to help students use the links?

Think about a recent topic you have taught: did you approach it in several different ways? have students met it before? how has this helped or hindered their understanding?

Approaching the curriculum as a network encourages the use of tasks designed to expose and exploit links within mathematics, and to encourage creativity. Students learn better if they can see connections between different parts of a subject and understand links between concepts as part of understanding the concepts themselves. Interconnectedness of mathematics and inclusivity of the curriculum are two main themes in this chapter.

> *Mathematics is a structure composed of a whole network of concepts and relationships, and, when being used, mathematics becomes a living process of creative activity* (NCC, 1989, A3 para 2.6)

Underpinning our planning is a view of school mathematics that recognizes and exploits interconnectedness and aims to make concepts accessible to all students from a wide range of mathematics. The challenge is to teach a concept such that *all* learners will have a chance to work at it. This means that it may not be necessary to separate students, offering each group a different curriculum.

Which topics in school mathematics are not taught to *all* students in your school? Why?

Making judgements about students' abilities in order to predict their potential for learning mathematics is a risky business. To some extent such judgements are self-fulfilling because the possibilities offered to students are then limited by teachers' expectations.

It is tempting, particularly if mathematics is seen as a linear hierarchy of concepts, to use some aspects of it as hurdles to be surmounted before certain other topics can be taught. One effect of curricular differentiation is that some students may not be taught trigonometry because they have earlier failed to do some aspect of arithmetic correctly, such as ratio, or failed to recall the names of angles, or how to use a protractor; this earlier failure may have placed them in a curriculum track in which trigonometry is not taught. In contrast, most mathematicians will admit to making mistakes with negative signs; fortunately they are not judged as weak but allowed to continue studying other topics. In one school a student who was able to transform traditional written alogrithms into a variety of own methods, and vice versa, was not allowed to work with the strongest students in the class because she 'kept reverting to her own methods' which, upon further investigation, were procedurally the same as traditional methods but set out more economically. Such decisions depend on a model of mathematics as a set of hurdles, rather than as a web of interrelated ideas about which learners' understanding grows in an individual fashion.

MATHEMATICS AS A CONNECTED WEB OF CONCEPTS

A fundamental aim of ours is to teach mathematics in ways that enable students to know and use its internal relationships. To put this belief into practice we plan individual lessons, groups of lessons based around one concept (which might include related skills, techniques, and knowledge) and whole schemes of work in ways that acknowledge this holistic view. The tasks we offer, the resources we use, the teaching strategies we adopt and the quality of the moment-by-moment interactions we have with individuals are the result of such planning. Having achieved a mathematical understanding, students ought to use and apply this knowledge in other contexts to make further links with concepts as yet unknown. To achieve this we build in opportunities for students to explore ideas and develop problem-solving approaches to their learning.

The school curriculum must be structured so that students can work on related concepts several times during their school lives. Meeting concepts in different ways, approaching them from different directions, gives more opportunities to learn than being taught them several times in much the same way. The student is thus enabled to return, apply, review and reconstrue from time to time. For example, in Year 7 students can be plotting number patterns that are linear, in Year 8 they can be looking at algebraic formulae for straight line graphs, and in Year 10 they may be looking at constant rates of change. They can look back at their previous work and suggest links for themselves, or have them pointed out by the teacher.

Creating a concept map

As an introduction to one possible planning method, we offer the following task:

Take two blank sheets of paper and in the middle of each piece of paper write the name of a mathematical topic such as 'volume', or 'ratio', or 'π'. Draw eight or nine rays coming from each word. At the end of each line write other concepts or pedagogic ideas that you would connect with your main topic.

For example if you have chosen 'volume', you might write *multi-link cubes* at the end of one line, *area* at another and *multiplying* at the end of another.

Are any of the new words on both pieces of paper similar? Would it be reasonable to connect words written on one sheet to those on another?

One could, for example, introduce π while students are making cylindrical boxes of a certain volume; they would need to know it and you could tell them about it when they needed it. Or π could be 'discovered' while working on ratios of lengths, being a ratio between the diameter and circumference. Or ratio could be explored through looking at dimensions, areas and volumes of similar solids.

Below is a map with Pythagoras' theorem at its centre. It is incomplete. We leave blanks to illustrate its use as a planning instrument to inform the teacher about other concepts that could be connected to Pythagoras. Students might be able to work with a variety of ideas while they develop their understanding of Pythagoras' theorem.

The figure maps out part of the mathematics curriculum and illustrates some connections between ideas. However, it is *our* links that are shown here. Students also make such connections for themselves, sometimes based on the flimsiest of reasons. For example, students have been known to confuse the formula for the area of a triangle with the formula for Pythagoras' relationship, presumably because they are both formulae about triangles, and both involve area and right angles. The teacher's job is to give opportunity to develop

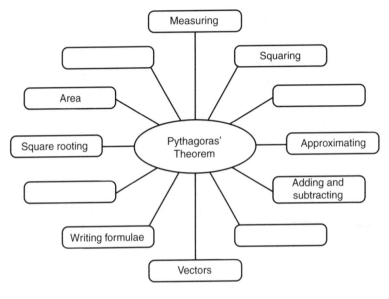

Fig. 3

helpful links, and those which reflect the structures of mathematics. Therefore, the construction of a scheme of work that recognizes and encourages the student's capacity to make links, but at the same time guides towards sensible links, is necessary to support holistic learning.

Later in the chapter we shall develop a group of lessons from the above diagram. Note that any of the aspects at the end of each ray could itself be the centre of another diagram.[1]

PLANNING FOR INTERCONNECTEDNESS

Whole schemes of work

For which parts of your scheme of work do you have professional autonomy?

Depending upon your position in school you may be able to influence the whole scheme of work, or only your individual lessons within a given scheme.

What aspects of your planning could you change and which would you want to change?

The construction of a scheme of work can be a unifying force for a mathematics department and a vehicle for professional development. Deciding what should be taught, when and to whom, requires discussion which will inevitably include teachers' beliefs about mathematics, students, and how students learn mathematics. One good-humoured way to do this is to select curriculum topics in random pairs and challenge each other to show how they can be linked. We would also include the requirement that all students can have access to the whole curriculum as an entitlement.

Department meetings can be a multi-purpose forum to discuss curriculum development, comparing lesson ideas, sharing anecdotes about success, for describing problems, and discussing ways to overcome difficulties.

One approach is to construct an outline plan, which splits the school year into a number of blocks of time. In one school the time blocks for Years 7 and 8 were about 2 weeks long; thus the scheme of work listed eighteen or so titles. In Y9, there were several 3-week time blocks and in Y10 and Y11 there were mainly 3- and 4-week blocks. Each block had a title which represented either a central concept, theme or forum in which ideas were based. So, for example, in Y7 a block titled 'Geoboards' was a collection of shape, space and measure tasks based upon a nine-pin geoboard (see below).

Another model is to identify major overarching themes in secondary mathematics. One school used mathematical aspects such as *Growth, Generalization, Position* and *Movement* as theme titles. They divided the school year into six half-termly modules within which related ideas in algebra, arithmetic and geometry were explored. Within each theme there were core elements of mathematical content and some optional and supportive elements.

	Number	Functions	Geometry
Growth	Multiplication and ratio; very large and very small numbers; number patterns	Steepness of straight lines and simple curves; exploring new functions on graphical calculators	Enlargements; similar shapes in two and three dimensions.
Position	Number line; large and small numbers on the number line; number patterns on coordinate grids	Four quadrants; loci; physical representations of functions; elementary sense of limits	Geometric constructions; bearings; definitions of position; vectors; trigonometry as a surveying tool.

Keeping track of the syllabus content was a matter of identifying and monitoring threads between modules and between years. The notion of a spiral curriculum in which students could revisit ideas from different perspectives, different directions at different times under-pinned this approach to planning. The table gives an idea of the kinds of connections that could be made within and across themes.

It can be seen that similar ideas are addressed from different viewpoints in the themes. For example, there is a link between the ratio work in Growth, similarity in Geometry, and trigonometry in Position. There is also a link between the graphs in Functions, the patterns in Position and the vectors and definitions of position in Geometry. In practice, planning was more complex than this, becoming a three-dimensional activity that also took account of the student's passage through school. The superimposition of national schemes of work can make this harder to achieve, but not impossible because:

> *Mathematics is not an arbitrary collection of disconnected items, but has a coherent structure in which various parts are inter-related. In very simple terms mathematics is about relationships.* (HMSO, 1985, p. 3)

We try to avoid a fragmented view of mathematics that does not allow for different styles of learning, nor for students' different constructions of knowledge, nor for following the students' own lines of enquiry.

In theme-based approaches each part of the scheme consists of a set of core tasks, possible developments and outline teacher notes. All teachers can add new ideas to the scheme. They can decide upon their own preferred approaches; the key idea is to work towards an agreed outline plan and to keep alive the processes of disseminating and sharing ideas.

Planning a module of work

Using a nine-pin geoboard as a starting point to illustrate the process of planning a sequence of lessons, the diagram below shows a sequence of questions about shape, space and measure which eventually are translated into a collection of tasks for students. The questions arise from considering what could be done using geoboards, and what sort of general things can be asked about the mathematical shapes that result, and how these might relate to the curriculum. In this case the tasks do not arise from concept maps, but from the stimulus of a mathematical resource. This illustrates another strategy for working with colleagues: that each teacher can consider possible mathematics stimulated by a resource and present it to the team.

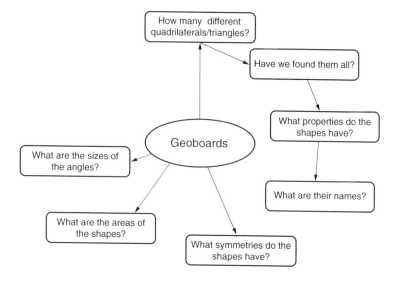

Fig. 4.

Each of these can be developed to different levels of complexity. For example, in working on sizes of angles, younger students could measure the angles with a protractor and older students could be asked to use trigonometry. The question, 'How many different quadrilaterals?', leads appropriately into discussions of geometric properties, congruence and transformations. The meaning of 'different' has to be sorted out and this leads to a notion of congruence. Also, a class could discuss whether a rhombus is a special case of a parallelogram, or whether all rectangles are similar in some way. Reflections, rotations and invariance could be explored. Students can try to demonstrate, explain and prove that all the possible shapes have been found. More and more layers of activity can be developed, none of which require the use of a textbook or worksheet. All the information is gathered by students who understand their mathematics by devising their own questions, using their own data and perspectives, and taking responsibility for what they do.

One way for students to devise questions is to identify constraints and variables in a mathematical situation, then change the variables within the constraints. For example: what if a 16-pin geoboard is used? What if we looked for pentagons, hexagons? What if we use an isometric geoboard? What if we use a three-dimensional (3-d) geoboard?

The geoboard ideas can provide students with at least a two-week sequence of lessons. Because of the open-ended nature of the task, individual students can work at different levels and depths; some might develop ideas of proof while others name shapes and find symmetries. Differentiated responses are built into the way the classroom works. Students are also expected and encouraged to work in an extended way. For instance, the answer to a question such as 'How many triangles are there?' is not just a number, but a number and a reason and, perhaps, a classification and some further questions. The teacher or other adult could prompt the development of mathematical argument by asking questions such as: 'How do you know you have got them all? How do you know you have not counted any of them twice?'

The teacher identifies key mathematical features and language, as they are needed, and includes some discussion and review of what has been met during the module. Thus the work done can be related to outside requirements.

Starting lessons

We use the words 'starting task' to describe the way a teacher introduces students to a new area of mathematics, a new situation to explore, a new mathematical space to work in. For some teachers and some models of teaching, 'lesson starter' can mean a short mental or oral task which may be a precursor to the main topic of the lesson, or may not be connected to the main content at all. In fact, all the ideas we present could be adapted to provide stimulation for mental work at the start of a lesson, but we are usually referring to what some teachers describe as 'the main part of the lesson'.

A good starting task should intrigue and motivate students and lead them to a rich network of mathematical concepts and techniques. The starting point is important for the effectiveness of future lessons and for the quality of students' learning experiences, but it is not enough on its own. Similar starting points can lead to very different lessons, not all of them rich in mathematical thinking and creativity. What is much more important is teachers' identification of the potential of a task to help develop students' understanding of mathematics. Also important is how this view is communicated to the students through interaction. Deciding upon a fertile point from which students will be able to learn mathematics is only one aspect of lesson planning; a further task is planning prompts and questions which encourage discussion of the central idea and others that might arise.

To plan in this way requires identification of key mathematical ideas, in pedagogic terms, and thought about how a student might come to understand them. In any class there will already exist a range of knowledge and past experiences about the concept – these are to be the main focus. Tasks ought to provide everyone with access to the basic idea, yet also open up avenues for further exploration by challenging preconceptions and intuitions of those students who are already familiar with the concept. For example, when working on fractions in secondary school it is useful to bear in mind that students will have had considerable past experience of halving and quartering imaginary cakes and pizzas, but probably little experience of treating fractions as an algebraic form, or as positions on a number line. Some starting points for fractions are offered in Chapter 14.

A starting lesson for work with geoboards

Experience shows that most students quickly interact with the equipment and, if provided with a short period of free exploration, will begin to pose problems for themselves and each other. (Others may ask the teacher what they are supposed to be doing!) Typical activities are: making different shapes; making a shape and asking a partner to make the same shape or a symmetrical one; naming shapes; trying to make the letters of the alphabet or the first nine counting numbers; making shapes that touch all the nine pins. Asking students where the mathematics is in their invented tasks can be revealing.

After a few minutes exploration, students can be asked to share what they have been doing and ideas can be recorded on the board. Often a student will describe a task similar to, and even identical to the one the teacher intended, i.e. 'How many different quadrilaterals can you make on the geoboard?' If such a question, or a similar one, does not arise, then it is up to the skill of the teacher to guide students more directly towards questions rich in mathematical potential.

A typical development is to invite students to come to the board, overhead projector, or large version of the geoboard and each draw one of their shapes on a separate grid. This is home-grown information around which to structure a whole class discussion. The teacher's aim is for students to share how many different shapes they have found, deciding what 'different' could mean, considering whether they have any shapes missing, what properties the shapes have, what their names are and so on. Any sense that producing the drawings, or counting them, is the end point of the work is openly challenged by critically questioning the results in teacher–class interaction.

Students then continue to work on explorations of the shapes, their properties, names, areas, angle sizes and perimeters. These results are the features listed in the curriculum, the outer layers that have been stripped away to find a mathematical arena in which students can work. The nine-pin geoboard provides students with opportunities to make these shapes within constraints; the practical nature of the equipment means they can touch, draw and argue about them. This type of activity is quite different to seeing the shapes in a book and then responding to a set of questions written by an author who is not a member of our own classroom.

Students' use of the chalkboard is common in many countries but has been relatively unusual in the UK. Possibly this is due to overanxiety about behaviour, and concerns about control, yet this technique is used effectively to involve students in schools where good behaviour cannot be taken for granted. One of us has used it frequently and effectively with low achieving adolescents in an inner city context. Interest in mathematics is increased and the request to contribute on the board is a statement of trust, to which, in our experience, the majority of adolescents respond well. Similar remarks could be made about the use of equipment.

A starting lesson for a sequence of work on straight line graphs

It is useful to look at another example of a starting lesson, this time for a mathematical topic: straight line graphs.

The school curriculum contains several topics which relate to straight line graphs and which might appear as a result of using a concept web: plotting points; understanding all quadrants; knowing which are the x and y axes; understanding linear algebraic expressions and equations; being able to state an algebraic rule for linear patterns in numbers; knowing about gradient and intercept; solving simultaneous linear equations; being able to reconstruct the equation of a straight line from various facts about it, and so on.

A central idea here is the representation of $y = mx + c$ (or some version of it) on the coordinate grid, so ways have to be found for students to explore the links between the formula and the grid. One way is to give formulae and plot them, graphical calculators and graph plotters being obvious ways to explore these without technical difficulties becoming demotivating obstacles. The teacher will have intentions about this task, and will select starting graphs which reveal useful features of this concept. For instance, it would be a good idea to start with families such as '$y = x, y = 2x, y = 3x$ ... now explore more of your own' or '$y = x, y = x + 1, y = x + 2, ...$' The mathematical power of controlling variables and asking 'What is the same and what is different?' is used to generate useful conjectures which can then be tested further. With this approach there is no need to offer students textbook exercises in order for them to work on these concepts.

A complementary way would be to develop the task given at the start of Chapter 4. Students choose four points on a coordinate grid which are in a line and look for patterns within and between the coordinate pairs. Finding common relationships between x and y

coordinates of the four points which lie on one line can lead to verbal versions of the appropriate formula, which then provide bridges to expressing the formula in algebra.[2] For example, the line expressed by

(1,4) ; (2,7) ; (3,10) ; (4,13)

might easily be described as 'add 3' but the same line expressed by

(1,4) ; (2,7) ; (4,13) ; (7,22)

is more likely to be described by relating x and y coordinates. If pairs are unequally spaced along the line, the temptation to express the generalization of the line in terms of adding rather than multiplying is avoided. Although this second set of coordinates appears to offer a more demanding problem, it usefully prevents students from focusing on the constant change of the y ordinates in relation to each other. Exploration can continue by asking students to give each other 'missing number' problems relating to the number pairs such as: (10,?), (?,31), which follow the same rule.

Of course, if the purpose of the task is to help students see how a constant change in the y ordinate provides the value of the multiplier acting upon the x ordinate (in this example, how the 'add 3 each time' relates to the 3 in $y = 3x + 1$), then the first set of coordinates might be chosen. Part of choosing a starting task is to decide how to help students focus on the features the teacher regards as central to understanding, and how to reduce being misled by other features.

Related tasks include: practising coordinates; extending lines outside the positive quadrant; plotting points which form a line parallel to some existing line; looking for similarities and differences between the relationships; plotting points which form a line at right angles to an existing line, and exploring the relationships; asking for lines which go through particular points; asking for lines with particular gradients.

One possibility that can be used with these complementary approaches is that half the class start one task and the others start the other. This gives the potential for some very rich discussion between students or as a whole class, relating the two approaches.

A well-known alternative starting point is the Function Game, usually played in silence, during which students are invited to uncover a function which is in the teacher's mind by contributing possible inputs and outputs.[3]

Planning a sequence of lessons

Students will learn different things from a sequence of lessons and it is likely that there will be as many different levels of understanding achieved as there are students in a class. Differentiation will occur, even with the most closely focused task. It is tempting to believe that doing a particular task ensures a particular kind of learning or achieves very specific understandings. It is possible, however, for a student to do a task and concentrate on features of it that do not highlight what the teacher has in mind.

For example, imagine asking students to identify certain number patterns as they appear on a number grid, such as 100-square, or a multiplication grid. It may be possible for some students to spot a spatial pattern and then spend their time colouring it, connecting these patterns neither to the numbers, nor to the size of the grid. The teacher needs to be aware that in cases like this, 'doing' may not lead to 'learning' without the intervention of questions about what is being done. These questions need to be planned in advance and discussed with other adults who may be helping in the classroom.

Differentiated learning is not always easy to spot. One can miss the point of an exercise while still getting right answers; for example a student might appear to correctly multiply by powers of ten using a personal rule about moving the decimal point when the teacher would prefer to use 'moving the digits'. In fact, moving the decimal point is an effective private strategy (we all have our own ways of recalling some algorithms!) but it does not make sense of the changing value of the digits as they move from one place to another. Alternatively, one can get wrong answers, yet go a long way towards understanding a principle in depth, such as when doing long division but getting a wrong answer solely due to a mistake in subtraction.

Differentiation must be taken into account when planning. Different responses and perceptions could, as in the straight line graph sequence given above, be positive factors in building a complex collection of ideas in the classroom. The sequence of lessons described below also illustrates this kind of differentiation; the main aim is to enable all students to arrive at some understanding of Pythagoras' theorem.

PYTHAGORAS

The starting task involves a whole-class introduction. The aim of this is to provide everyone with a common experience, something with which they can all get involved, then begin to develop according to their existing knowledge, perceptions and preferred styles of learning. At the outset to the topic everyone is included and no decision is taken by the teacher about who may or may not be able to understand the central concept. Indeed, there is an expectation that everyone will understand it, although perhaps to different depths.

One can begin by asking students to describe a given line segment on a square grid; the line is neither vertical nor horizontal. The whole-class discussion develops using different strategies such as asking everyone to write down some information about the line or discuss in pairs how best to describe the line. Students fit their own version of a vector description to the line and then consider how to draw a square using that line as one side of it.

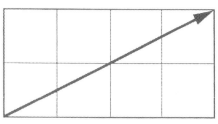

Fig. 5.

The whole class approach is used to establish a series of tasks for the students to work on, either individually, in pairs or in small groups: draw a selection of lines, then describe each as a vector. Students could describe the other three sides of the square using vector notation, or get straight to the heart of the concept, finding ways of calculating the area of the square using a connection between area of the square and its vector components. Since this last idea involves squaring numbers and adding, it is unlikely that students will see the relationship unless they have a wide range of experience in expressing generalities algebraically. Classes who have limited experience of pattern spotting are unlikely to see this unless someone in the class has prior knowledge of Pythagoras and is able to pass the message around! Students can be directed towards the desired relationship through a preparatory activity discovering which numbers can, and which cannot, be made by adding the squares of two integers.

Students' construction of Pythagoras' theorem will develop at different rates. By the end of the introductory lesson there will be a range of outcomes; some students will be able to verbalize and write down Pythagoras' procedure, others will find drawing and describing 'slanted' squares a challenge. For the remainder of the module it may be tempting to avoid whole class teaching, but this denies some of the class the opportunity to see further possibilities in the topic. Students might be directed by the teacher to work on any of the following tasks:

- describing the four vectors that form each square they have drawn;
- commenting on similarities and differences in the vectors;
- calculating the area of each square;

- connecting the area of the square with the components of the vector;
- writing this connection in words or as a formula;
- writing this formula as a program on a graphic calculator;
- translating this knowledge to right-angled triangles, where the length of the vector is equivalent to the hypotenuse;
- checking the calculation works for non-integer lengths;
- seeing what happens when non-right-angled triangles are used;
- transferring their knowledge to different situations, such as working out the lengths of lines on a nine-pin geoboard or the diagonals of familiar rectangular objects;
- carrying out problems in 3-d, such as the length of the 3-d diagonal through different sized cuboids made from multi-link cubes.

The list describes the teachers' intentions, but also models an investigative approach to mathematics. If the class is used to investigating mathematics they may think of doing some of these tasks themselves. By the end of the module each student will have constructed ways of understanding aspects of Pythagoras' theorem. However, without further whole class discussions there is little opportunity, unless the teacher deliberately puts students in touch with each other, to share the ideas that are being pursued in the classroom. Reports of work done and presentations of results can become a regular feature of lessons during which students can see the progress they could make, relative to their current work.

We are not recommending the particular task-sequences above as *recipes* for best ways of teaching topics. For example, another method of introducing students to Pythagoras' theorem, which is also accessible to all, is for students to draw random triangles, construct squares on the sides and add the two smaller areas. A collection of the results is put on the board, some triangles giving the result that the sum of the two smaller squares is greater than the third square, others that the sum is smaller. The teacher then poses a question (if an alert student has not already done so) about when the sum will be equal to the third square. Pythagoras' relationship becomes a surprise special case which might intrigue students.[4]

INCLUSIVITY, EXPECTATIONS AND EQUALITY OF OPPORTUNITY

> *Equality of opportunity is one of a broad set of common values and purposes which underpin the school curriculum.* (David Blunkett: Foreword to the English National Curriculum for Mathematics, 1999)

Inclusivity and expectations are strongly linked to equality of opportunity. All children, no matter what they have achieved in the past, have contributions to make in present and future lessons. A teacher who values and uses the inevitably wide range of student contributions enables all to be included and is likely to become more and more skilled at devising ways to help all understand the concept under consideration.

Student inclusivity is achieved by developing a core curriculum that can be extended. Exclusion results from deleting parts of the curriculum for some students. We suggest a planning process that includes:

- construction of modules within coherent internal conceptual connections;
- decisions about the specific skills and knowledge students would need and meet within each module;
- identification of accessible and interesting starting points;
- construction of extension tasks for each module;
- determination of useful resources for each module.

But this is only part of the story. The teacher's intentions have to be transformed into interactive strategies, nurturing learning and prompting mathematical thinking, turning the designed curriculum into mathematical learning.

In your opinion, do our ideas offer usable frameworks for achieving equality of opportunity?

SUMMARY

In this chapter we have demonstrated some methods of curriculum design which take account of the interconnected nature of mathematics and recognize the different ways students learn. We have considered the importance of short, medium and long-term lesson and module planning from the perspectives of entitlement to a common curriculum for students and professional development of teachers. We have illustrated how these issues can be embraced through, for example, the use of practical equipment and by looking at different approaches to teaching specific concepts such as straight line graphs and Pythagoras' theorem.

We have completed this chapter by looking at how student inclusion is linked to equality of opportunity and differentiated teaching and learning. Curriculum planning which *responds to* (rather than *results in*) differentiated learning, in the ways we have described, provides access to learners' mathematical entitlement.

NOTES

1. In Perks and Prestage (1994) further, similar, diagrams are used for more detailed aspects of lesson planning.
2. See *In Our Classrooms* (1993).
3. A description of this can be found in Banwell *et al.* (1986) pp.90–91.
4. This is from an idea by Movshovitz-Hadar (1988)

REFERENCES

Baker, L. *et al.* (1992) *Using Geoboards.* Derby: Association of Teachers of Mathematics

Banwell, C., Saunders, K. and Tahta, D. (1986) *Starting Points.* Diss: Tarquin.

Brown, L. *et al.* (1993) *In Our Classrooms.* Derby: Association of Teachers of Mathematics

HMSO (1985) *Mathematics from 5 to 16.* London: Her Majesty's Stationery Office

Perks, P. and Prestage, S. (1994) 'Planning for learning', in B. Jaworski and A. Watson (eds) *Mentoring in Mathematics Teaching.* London: Falmer.

Movshovitz-Hadar, N. (1988) 'Stimulating presentation of theorems followed by responsive proofs'. *For the Learning of Mathematics,* 8, 2. pp. 12–30.

NCC (1989) see Chapter 4 for the full reference.

—6—
Working together

In this chapter we describe a shared approach to developing mathematics teaching, and the responsibility of curriculum leadership. We discuss strategies for supporting and inducting new teachers and learning support assistants into the department. Finally, there is a very brief section on initiating contact with parents and governors.

SHARING LESSON IDEAS

You may like to do the following:

In the next five minutes write down the favourite 'good' ideas that you use for teaching mathematics

and

Briefly write down how you usually approach teaching an aspect of shape, or geometry, with Y7, Y9 and Y11 classes.

These are intended to be different types of questions. The first question starts from interesting ideas and, subsequently, the intended areas of curriculum content are considered. The second question begins with an area of curriculum content and asks you to consider what tasks you use to enable students to access the desired content.

The first part of this chapter will assume a task-oriented approach to teaching mathematics, and hence deals with the recognition and sharing of potentially rich starting points and ideas. Another approach, based on analysis of different images and views of learning, will be discussed later. However, what we say meanwhile about the development of a culture of sharing in mathematics departments applies to a variety of curriculum approaches.

A 'good' idea

An example of a 'good' idea, in response to the first question, might be one that engages students in a range of curriculum content. For example:

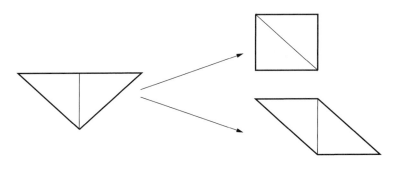

Fig. 6.

Take an isosceles right angled triangle and cut it in half down its line of symmetry.

Before going further it may be interesting to consider what shapes can be made by joining edges of the same length using the new shapes formed. This in turn could lead to students looking at how different shapes can be formed from a dissection of the original isosceles right-angled triangle, conservation of area, the properties and the similarities and differences of the new shapes. By fitting together the two half-size triangles formed from the first cut, a square and a parallelogram can be formed. Note that the areas are the same but the perimeters are different.

Now start again with another triangle the same size as the first one. Fold it down the line of symmetry, then cut this folded shape down the 'new' line of symmetry.

What happens as more folds are made before the shape is cut in half?

These are further questions that might be posed, together with the intended areas of content:

Questions	Mathematical content
How many pieces are made?	Number sequences
What shapes are they?	Properties, names and similar shapes
What fraction of the areas of each of these shapes in comparison with the area of the original triangle?	Fractions with denominators of 2^n
	Conservation of area
Can the shapes be rearranged back to the original triangle?	Symmetry
What are the total perimeters of the pieces?	Measure, possibly involving the use Pythagoras' theorem.

In deciding to use this task, different teaching strategies might be considered. For instance, the students could be set the task of seeing for themselves what happens when the original triangle is folded twice, three times and so on, before being cut down the final line of symmetry. Alternatively the teacher might keep control of the folding and the cutting and initially ask students to visualize and draw what they think each resulting set of shapes will be, before revealing the answer in a whole class setting. Further, students may pose their own questions about shapes.

Discussion of this task reveals the importance of considering resources, teaching strategies, curriculum content and learning styles.

SHARING RESOURCES, TEACHING STRATEGIES, LEARNING STYLES AND CURRICULUM CONTENT

In structuring a scheme of work resource issues need to be taken into account; the use of a wide range of resources has implications for the budget. If money is to be spent on resources such as: coloured paper, a wide variety of grid papers, glue, scissors, sugar paper, ATM mats,[1] pegs and pegboards, multi-link cubes, geoboards and rubber bands, geostrips, playing cards, dominoes, a guillotine, Cuisenaire rods, counters, dice, scales and tape measures, this will impact upon the purchase of other major items of expenditure, such as textbooks. Accordingly, decisions about which resources need to be bought have to be taken with teaching style and curriculum structure in mind.

Think of an area of mathematics which you find difficult to teach. What sort of resources could help? What are the essential features of these resources and can they be acquired cheaply?

Think of a maths resource. How might you use it with Y7, Y9, Y11?

Of course not all resources need to be bought from manufacturers; some can be acquired for minimal cost. For instance by gathering together large amounts of scrap plywood or blockboard (your local woodyard might give you any amount of this), some 25 mm nails and a couple of pots of paint, it is possible to make whole class sets of various types of geoboards. Whilst you are looking around for the wood you might also see if there are any scrap pieces of pegboard! In order to get hold of free packs of cards you might ring a local Bridge Club and ask what they do with their used packs. As for elastic bands, the school secretary might save all the bands from the postal deliveries for you; whilst you are asking for these there might be lots of strong brown envelopes too that can be used for carrying out sampling experiments. Liaison with the school's design and technology department might be beneficial. Students could work on a joint project designing, making and suggesting uses for mathematical equipment.

We are not suggesting a resources-led curriculum, but recognize that teachers who are in the habit of asking mathematical questions will often use equipment as catalysts for devising tasks. Making use of time in department meetings for colleagues to describe how they have used certain resources in their teaching can be valuable. We offer some outline suggestions for resource use below.

Task	Equipment	Mathematics
Finding all the triangles and quadrilaterals on a 3 by 3 dot grid.	Nine-pin geoboards and nine-dot grid paper.	Classifying triangles and quadrilaterals; area of shapes; angle sizes.
Paper folding.	A4 paper.	Properties of shapes; tessellating shapes; angles; using algebra to define area and perimeter
Constructing 3-d shapes	ATM mats, Glue.	Making Platonic and Archimedean solids; Euler's theorem; truncating solids.
Exploring numbers on a 100-square.	OHP and 100-square grid paper.	Mental arithmetic; times tables; algebra.
Finding all the cuboids with a fixed number of cubes.	Multi-link cubes, isometric grid paper.	Dimensions; volume; surface area; prime numbers; constructing formulae.
Exploring ways to choose four dots in a line within certain size grid.	Pegs and pegboards.	Co-ordinates; vectors; Pythagoras' theorem.

and . . .

Look at a piece of A4 paper and seeing how many mathematical questions you can ask about it as you turn it around, fold it, cut it and so on.

SHARING IDEAS

Having found or designed a 'new' task, tried it out with one or two classes, evaluated the effectiveness of the idea in relation to students' responses, achievements and mathematical development, it will be useful to share the idea with colleagues. In view of the busy nature of teaching, we should ask:

When you come across a 'new' idea for the mathematics classroom, how do you share it with colleagues?

Ideas are shared informally or during meetings. In one school the department meeting agenda is always about the doing, teaching and learning of mathematics, and administrative chores are dealt with on paper. Sadly, most departments feel so overwhelmed with organizational and management details they feel unable to use their meetings in this way.

   Another possibility might be that, during the process of trying the idea out with one of your classes, you involve a colleague to spend, say, fifteen minutes observing what you do with your class. Arising from such situations there are potentially two clear benefits: your colleague can gain first-hand access to a new idea; and you can receive some valuable feedback on your teaching. Alternatively, if this is not possible, you could: write a brief synopsis of what occurred in the lesson and share this with colleagues; take a photocopy of the work of one of your students and share this; choose a time when you are not timetabled to teach and ask a colleague if you might introduce the idea to one of their classes.

   One difficulty of sharing 'good' ideas is that we might find that everyone uses it with all of their classes. For instance, when an idea called 'Frogs'[2] was first suggested in 1976 to the department where one author worked, every teacher did it with every class! 'Good' ideas are those that open up opportunities for outcomes ranging from practice of techniques to higher level abstract generalizations; thus they ought to be accessible to a wide age range of students. But when you come to introduce an idea the following year with a new (to you) group, there is a chorus from the class of: '. . . but we did this last year with Mr So and So!' One approach is to say, at the beginning of a lesson, 'I know you have seen this idea before . . .' and to go on to emphasize that there are so many directions in which exploration can go that no one needs to repeat previous work.

   With a task-based curriculum, one approach to sharing is to reach agreement with colleagues about the use of ideas; thus should a colleague decide it would be useful to revisit and develop an idea with an older age group, she will know there is the likelihood that the class may well have met the particular starting point before. The issue can be discussed with students, showing that the expectation is that they should not repeat their previous approaches. They could be encouraged to find their previous work and develop new starting points from it.

A further approach to sharing teaching in a task-based curriculum would be to talk about what students learnt through the task, and to be explicit about how the teacher structured the work and the interactions in order to enable such learning to take place. It is also worth noting that what seems to be a 'good' idea for one teacher may not be 'good' for another. With some classes 'Frogs' can be used to generate coloured wall displays, simple results and delightful or dubious notation systems; in other hands it can be the starting point for an understanding of quadratic structure. More important than the task itself is what it means for a teacher to *use* it, and for a class to *do* it. Teachers may explore the mathematical potential of a new task, but the issue is how students might be guided to engage with these potentials.

In one school, all students in one year were asked to work on situations which had been constructed by the teachers to illustrate the relationship: $y = 3x + 1$. All students were given printed coordinate grids on which to plot their results, so that their final graphs were identical, even though they appeared to have been working on very different tasks. The agreement among the teachers was that the graphs would be displayed and students would discuss why they were the same, thus *having* to explore the reasons why the gradient was 3 and the intercept 1. In this case, the tasks were structured to lead all students to reflect on the underlying structure of the mathematical relationship. In one class, however, the lesson ended with separate posters being made to describe the work done, and no class discussion of similarities. While other students were being praised for generalizing their results and relating the gradient to the original situations, students in the last group were being praised for the presentation of their work.

Often tasks can be superficially 'finished' with the production of a diagram and a formula, and a vague sense of having done some logical or strategic thinking, with the specific mathematical content unexplored.

SHARING STRATEGIES

A different approach is to identify ways of teaching which, rather than leading to deliberately varied outcomes, seems to enable most students to grasp a core technique, concept or idea. In other words, teachers could share strategies rather than task ideas. One example of this kind of almost-universally 'good' approach is to represent multiplication using a grid.

	300	20	6
60	18000	1200	360
7	2100	140	42

Students need to know single digit multiplication facts and how to operate with powers of ten. This layout provides a good introduction to distributivity, which plays a large part in algebra in secondary schools.

Another 'good' approach is a silent introduction in which students watch and contribute to an unfolding mathematical story on the board, silently making sense of what they see. The whole class may be trying to make sense of a tightly focused task, such as the development of a sequence to illustrate multiplying brackets:

$$2 (1 + 2) = 2 + 4 = 6$$
$$2 (2 + 3) = 4 + 6 = 10$$
$$2 (3 + 4) = 6 + 8 = 14$$

and so on.

As students reach an understanding of what they see, they can come to the board and contribute to the story. There will still be variation of outcome in terms of what is learnt, but not in terms of what has been explored. (Extending this sequence, and many other sequences, upwards rather than downwards can force a class to consider negative numbers in an interesting way!)

These two examples suggest different approaches to sharing strategies. In the first case, teachers can demonstrate the technique to colleagues who have not seen it before. In the second case, it is more likely that teachers would prefer to see a lesson in action, with all its management implications, than to have only a verbal description.

So far, we have assumed that mathematics is taught inclusively through a sequence of tasks chosen to provide opportunities to work on situations in various ways: through exploration, practice, generalization, abstraction, eventually relating what is construed to conventional forms of mathematics.

SHARING IMAGES

One approach that benefits from team discussion, and which is also inclusive and not dependent on textbooks, is to identify features of the mathematics to be taught and to discuss what kinds of models, images, metaphors, examples, questions and methods are most likely to help students understand them. For instance, when discussing equivalent fractions as a basis for all fraction work, one teacher might report saying 'what you do to the top you do to the bottom'. In a collegiate atmosphere it would be the responsibility of other teachers to ask her what she says about adding and subtracting to the 'tops' and 'bottoms', because students may believe these to be permissible. Other teachers may report using calculators to show decimal representation of fractions, or using some kind of physical model to show equivalence, or dividing up a unit strip into families of fractions and seeing which coincide, or representing fractions as ordered pairs on a coordinate grid to show the relationship between them, and so on (see Chapter 14). Discussion of these very different ways of seeing equivalence, and learning about them, enriches everyone's practice. Different beliefs are implicit in the different approaches and teachers might try each other's images and metaphors to see which combination of approaches makes most sense to them and their students.

Another example is the sharing of approaches to percentages. One teacher might work at simple calculations which can be combined to give more complex percentages: using tenths, hundredths, halving and doubling and so on. Another may emphasize language, saying that

5 per cent of 62

means

5 per (meaning divide) cent (meaning 100) of (meaning multiply) 62.

Another may ask students to collect discount advertisements from local papers and then show them the techniques they will need to find out which is the best bargain. Another may pose a problem such as:

Which is better, 17% tax on a price which has 10% discount or a 10% discount off a price which includes 17% tax?

Again, each approach shows different beliefs about mathematics, students, motivation and learning.

While new teachers may have several chances to discuss these matters, experienced teachers may not be able to find the time to do so unless the mathematics department deliberately makes space for pedagogic matters in its meetings.

SHARED CONSTRUCTION OF A SCHEME OF WORK

Of course it would be wholly impractical for colleagues to hold all curriculum information in their heads and for this reason it is important that ideas and starting points are detailed in a scheme of work to inform and support colleagues' practices.

Reaching agreement with colleagues over a scheme of work involves the head of department in a key managerial role. Initially all the 'good' ideas that colleagues know about need to be collected together and this information can be fed into a year-by-year curriculum framework. To do this, members of the department can use departmental meeting time either to list ideas based upon different concepts, perhaps using a current national curriculum framework, or to work from the perspective of students' year-by-year development and decide where ideas might most appropriately fit. This process requires time, but the resulting commitment of department members to the final outcome is important.

Structuring ideas into the scheme of work and finding ways of disseminating an agreed structure are next steps. This might seem to be a mammoth task. However, once a basic structure exists, then updating need only occur on a yearly basis, so that any new ideas that colleagues have tried with their classes can be built in to the following year's scheme of work. One head of department collected a record of impressions, difficulties and colleagues' comments throughout the year to inform this process. In this way the scheme of work becomes an agreed, shared, changing and dynamic document idiosyncratic to the department. This is clearly a different model to one where the main responsibility for writing a scheme of work is given over to the head of department, or alternatively, where the scheme of work is predominantly scheme or textbook driven. In the model described, the head of department is managing the development and production of the scheme of work, and the ideas contained within are produced cooperatively by the whole department.

Using the environment

As well as ideas, resources and strategies members of a department may also wish to share different ways of arranging classrooms and some of the different purposes to which these arrangements might be put. Before offering some ways we have used different furniture arrangements, and the purposes of them, consider the following:

Think about and write down the different arrangements of the classroom furniture that you have used in the last 6 months; for each of these write about a particular way of working that was most suited to each arrangement.

Here are some different furniture arrangements and the uses to which they might be put:

Furniture arrangement	Purpose
Desks in rows	So everyone can face the 'front' to receive specific, detailed instructions
Desks separated	For individual work or for tests
Desks in blocks	For group work
Desks in a 'U' shape	To convey a 'conference' effect and enable discussion
Chairs in two or three arcs around the board/screen (desks pushed to the back of the room)	For a whole class discussion which requires students to have access to the board
Chairs in one ring	For a whole class discussion which does not require students to have access to the board, and in which the teacher is an almost-equal participant Also for certain whole class activities such as making polygons with a ball of string, or placing kebab sticks to make a shape with the largest possible area
No chairs or desks (using the school hall or working outside)	For physical activity, such as 'acting out loci' problems

HELPING NEW TEACHERS

Developing a scheme of work in a shared fashion is important for everyone's personal development. The process of curriculum planning through negotiation contributes to the departmental culture. When a new teacher comes to the department the culture is bound to alter slightly as this person will bring their attitudes and preferred ways of working to the department. Equally the new teacher needs to be inducted into the ways of the department.

New members of department come in with several backgrounds. They could be: newly qualified; experienced in another school; appointed to a post of responsibility; covering someone's leave; or mainly teaching another subject. Whatever the nature of this new-to-the-department teacher, she will require induction at some level and intensity.

Whoever is in charge of induction will carry out the role according to the beliefs and values they have about mathematics teaching. Indeed, the impact our beliefs and values have upon the way we describe our teaching is significant. However, it is hard to be explicit, even to ourselves; much of our knowledge of how to teach is tacit and only comes to mind when, in the heat of the moment, we decide what to do. To see how well you can identify your beliefs and values, try this:

In the next five minutes write down the most important beliefs and values you have about teaching mathematics.

If possible ask colleagues to do the same and then compare responses.

Providing a new teacher with the departmental scheme of work is the basic minimum requirement. But the new teacher will also need to be inducted into the ethos of the department and the underlying pedagogical ideas which influence the way mathematics is viewed, taught and learnt. Of course the new teacher will have much to offer and will bring their own teaching styles and ideas. The teacher who is given the responsibility for induction, therefore, has a further key role to play in disseminating the culture of the department and simultaneously embracing what the new teacher has to offer. This is not a short-term task or obligation; indeed, in working with colleagues in an evolving department the process is ongoing and never ending.

The issue about use of time to induct new members of staff into the department must also be considered. This might be achieved by spending time supporting her in lessons, or inviting the new teacher into the classes of experienced teachers. Agreeing upon a time to meet, on a regular basis, to discuss progress and difficulties is essential. It is also important that such discussions, while inevitably including information about settling in, organization, and being a professional colleague, should also focus on the learning of mathematics, particularly if the previous experience has been of a different style of teaching.

Induction can be a difficult balancing act, particularly if the new teacher has fairly strong ideas about approaches to teaching and some of these are in contrast to the department pedagogy. One excellent strategy is to find time for working on mathematics as a team in the department meetings. This reminds teachers of their central purpose, and also provides opportunity to discuss differences of view and approach within the teaching team. Another significant way for teachers of mathematics to share ideas and engage with others on issues of personal and curriculum development at a national level is through membership of the professional associations.[3] These bodies, through their journals, publications, conferences and local branch meetings, provide teachers with enormous opportunities for sharing ideas, discussing pedagogy and enhancing teaching.

Newly qualified teachers

Try to cast your mind back to your first lesson or your first week as a secondary mathematics teacher. What memories and images come to mind?

The type of support required for newly qualified teachers (NQTs) should take into account that they may only be a few months away from their training and will need good quality induction and careful support. In terms of finding out about schemes of work, resources, departmental approaches to assessment, numeracy policies, grouping arrangements and many other issues, their needs are similar to those of anyone joining the department, but in other respects their needs will be context-dependent in terms of the skills they have begun to develop and those they must acquire.

The head of mathematics has a responsibility for finding out what these needs are. There are a number of possible ways of doing this such as: asking the NQT to talk about her best few lessons; analysing any different teaching strategies she has developed in comparison with those prevalent in the department; asking her what kinds of resources she has used and comparing these with a list of departmental resources. Perhaps there is a department handbook through which she can identify issues which need elaboration or discussion. Finding out what the NQT has to offer, in terms of her strengths and needs, may have begun during the interview for the post.

In some schools it is possible for experienced teachers to observe the NQT teaching during the first year. The model of being observed and assessed may be a familiar one during training, but when in a first job it may be more helpful to plan a lesson and team-teach it with an experienced teacher. In this way, the departmental ethos and knowledge of ways to work in the particular school are more easily understood. This is especially important for teachers whose first job is in a very different kind of school than those in which they trained. For example, a student who trained in a school with rigid setting and set textbooks but who goes to work in a mixed-ability school with an activity-based scheme of work, or vice versa, will need a lot of support and help to develop planning and teaching strategies.

INVOLVING LEARNING SUPPORT ASSISTANTS

Although the training and roles of a learning support assistant (LSA) are different to those of an NQT, many of the induction needs listed above will be identical. However, a LSA is likely to spend time in a range of different teachers' classrooms and therefore has to learn how to adapt to a range of different expectations and expertise. Key considerations are to identify what are the LSA's strengths and roles and how to best utilize these strengths to carry out specific roles.

Aims and roles of the learning support assistant

What do you consider to be the main aims and roles of a LSA?

Think about the last time you had LSAs in your classroom. What did they do? What did you expect them to do? Are the answers to these two questions the same?

Who is responsible for deciding how the LSA might best utilize his time in your classroom?

Forming an agreed understanding of the complementary aims and roles of the LSA, the teachers and those students requiring extra support is important. Ideally discussion could take place before the lesson between the teacher and the LSA and as a result the LSA is aware of the teacher's intentions and can decide how best to help the student. When the teacher carries out some whole class teaching, the LSA can contribute in some agreed way and is able to enhance the learning environment.

The LSA could decide when it is useful to sit next to the student requiring learning support. He should interpret the teacher's questions and intentions in such a way that the challenge for the student of working on the mathematics is maintained. Seeing particular students struggle with something, the LSA could find ways of helping the student without doing it for them. It is interesting to ask LSAs to be aware of who uses the pen when working one-to-one with a student, and whether such use is supporting the student, or has the effect of simplifying or complexifying the work.

The main issue is how support time can be utilized to greatest effect. What understandings and expectations exist between class teacher and support assistant and, of greatest importance, what understandings and expectations exist between the support assistant and the student(s) for whom the support is primarily intended? As with most accepted practices in school mathematics we are arguing for norms to be questioned, for normal practices to be re-assessed against criteria of equity and inclusion.

Discussion between LSAs and teachers could take place in a department meeting to decide upon roles, responsibilities and expectations in general. Articulation of general aims and roles, and how they might be most effectively carried out, will provide the basis for effective learning support.

Supporting individual students

Determining more specific roles relating to particular individuals' needs and the intended mathematical content of a lesson requires different types of planning. Over time a LSA will build a picture of a student's needs and how they might most effectively be met within a planned scheme of work. It is often the case that weaker students are directed towards simple, repetitive 'basic' tasks by LSAs and hence excluded from the lesson. However, if the aims of an activity are not discussed with LSAs, this approach may be the only one they know. In UK there is often talk of 'brighter' students being 'held back' in mixed-ability classes. Weaker students can also be held back by inappropriate use of support and reduction of challenge. To avoid this effect, LSAs develop strategies which enable particular students to take a full part in lessons. Some of these strategies might be generic, and the LSA, through contact with students in other subjects, might be the best-placed person to develop these; others may be specific to mathematics and can only be developed alongside subject specialists.

Other roles

Consideration of wider and other specific roles for LSAs raises further questions and possibilities. For example:

In a whole class discussion how might another adult in your classroom add to the classroom atmosphere?

Would there be any benefit of one adult playing the 'devil's advocate' role, or asking 'difficult' question in class?

Using questioning techniques to reveal what a student understands and to help develop their understanding is a key strategy and applicable to all learners; like a teacher, a LSA needs a repertoire of general questions to ask such as: What do you think you are being asked to do? What part of the introduction to the lesson did you understand? What questions do you have about the work? What do you understand about the work?

A student with special educational needs is on the same continuum of learning as any other student; the manner in which learning happens will not necessarily be an expected response to a particular question or action of the teacher. Learning takes place as a consequence of events, thoughts, unravellings, suggestions, refutations, confirmations, practice and consolidation. Trying to identify the exact point in time when any student gained an understanding of, for example, Pythagoras' theorem, is wholly problematic. Indeed it may not be until the student automatically decides to use Pythagoras' theorem in a non-obvious or unexpected context that the student and the teacher can be confident the rule is understood. It is necessary to recognize that the learner with special educational needs is as much in need of having space and time to learn as of having direct help and support. One teacher told us:

Some people would say that Donna is a slow learner. I don't agree. When she learns, she learns just as quickly as anyone else. She just does it less frequently.

In practice, this means that LSAs may have to try out some mathematical tasks for themselves in order to understand the mathematics and to experience how the expectations of the teacher might be met by students. Without this kind of experience one could have a situation in which the teacher expects students to be looking for generalizations of number patterns, but the supported student is being helped to learn some multiplication tables which have provided an obstacle to the generation of the patterns. The supported student then misses out on the experience of the rest of the class in discussing what can be seen when several examples have been done, thus also missing an opportunity to generalize from the patterns. All involved have been working with good intentions, but the result is a student who is effectively excluded from the whole class experience. Information about the student's problems with multiplication is needed by the teacher, and the LSA will have expert knowledge of this kind of detail, but the LSA needs the access to the teacher's expert knowledge of ways to avoid, or smooth over, obstacles to the main intention of the lesson.

Inclusion is more than a matter of physical location in the classroom, or of soaking up the social atmosphere, and LSAs have a key role in enabling curriculum inclusion in mathematics.

INVOLVING PARENTS AND GOVERNORS

Introducing parents and governors to the ways mathematics is taught by demonstrating some of the pedagogic principles is a valuable way of involving the wider community in education.

One way to achieve this is to hold mathematics evenings for parents and governors. There are different formats that might be used, such as:

- a carousel method, where visitors move between several rooms and are provided with outline versions of typical lessons;
- a workshop, set up in one large room or hall, where a wide range of problems are provided and teachers are available to offer support, initiate discussion and answer questions;
- to separate visitors into groups attached to a teacher for a full 'lesson' exploring a mathematical situation.

A plenary session is useful to bring everyone together to share experiences and discuss implications of the ways they, and students, learn mathematics.

Our experience shows that evenings can be very beneficial and can generate useful discussion about ways to support students' mathematical development and the professional development of the department. They also help to avoid misunderstandings which can arise between a department and parents and governors whose only other source of information might be the media.

SUMMARY

This chapter has focused on collecting good ideas for teaching mathematics and sharing practice. We have taken into consideration issues such as different arrangements of classroom furniture and a range of resources available to enhance students' learning opportunities.

We have discussed the importance of studying one's own beliefs and values, about teaching mathematics, ways of working and curriculum planning, in preparation for inducting new teachers, trainee teachers and learning support assistants, parents and governors into the department's ways of working.

NOTES

1. These are inexpensive card polygonal shapes, known as Mathematical Activity Tiles, obtainable from Association of Teachers of Mathematics, www.atm.org.
2. This idea involves finding the minimum number of moves, according to certain rules, which will transfer 'frogs' from 'lily pads' on one side of a gap to lily pads the other side. See Hardy, Haworth and Love (1983).
3. In the UK the professional associations are Association of Teachers of Mathematics and the Mathematical Association.

REFERENCES

Hardy, T., Haworth, A. and Love, E. (1983) *Points of Departure 2*. Derby: Association of Teachers of Mathematics. This is one of a series of four booklets which contain hundreds of investigative starting points.

—7

Assessment as an integral part of teaching mathematics

The introduction of new methods of assessment in mathematics may disguise the fact that *all* teachers are assessors and always have been. At a most informal, fundamental level teachers assess students as part of getting to know them, make judgements about students by observing types of response, behaviour, mistakes, communication skills and many other ordinary classroom actions and events. These judgements help decide how to respond, what sort of challenges to offer and how to adapt teaching to individuals. They also influence expectations of students, and responses to students may therefore become habitual.

During the last two decades more attention has been given to assessment as a way of monitoring educational standards in general and giving information about the progress of individuals. This has led to the use of new forms of assessment fitting new attitudes to mathematics more closely than timed tests might do. For example, in the UK national assessment structures currently include the requirement for extended, exploratory tasks to be undertaken and assessed. A project in the Netherlands designs holistic assessment tasks which require students to use mathematics to solve a complex problem given in a context. In some parts of the world students provide a balanced portfolio of their mathematical work for assessment purposes.

It has been known for some time that timed tests in mathematics disadvantage some students who can, nevertheless, show creditable understanding of mathematics in other contexts, so new forms of assessment should give more students the chance to show what they can do. At the same time, the requirement that students will be assessed in new ways puts an obligation on the teacher to teach in ways which will allow them to succeed. In other words, the assessment requirements are used as standards for planning the curriculum and how it is taught.

There ought to be a two-way relationship between the curriculum and the assessment methods, so that changes in the curriculum are reflected through assessment, and changes in assessment are reflected in the curriculum. 'Teaching to the test' is a rather derogatory way to describe the classroom manifestation of this two-way relationship, but failure to take the nature of the test into account can disadvantage students. There is a fine line to be taken between treating students justly by fully preparing them for the tests they will have to face, and ensuring that this does not degenerate into the kind of test-training which fails to give them a love for the subject, or a foundation on which to build further study. Students with a marketplace view of education may also see little worth in mathematical activity which does not seem to relate to assessment. Teachers' own assessment procedures are likely to relate closely to what is taught and the way it is taught. Externally imposed assessment structures may not match students' classroom experience, so that they may be tested with forms of question which they have never encountered. They may also be expected to answer questions in unfamiliar ways, such as giving reasons for results or suggesting alternative methods.

How do you prepare students for external assessments through your usual teaching? Do you prepare them in any special ways just before the assessment, e.g. with memory aids or examination tricks?

What mismatches exist between your teaching and the implications of assessment procedures, and how do you handle these?

In this chapter we focus on assessment as a relationship between teacher and student, teacher and class, as an activity embedded in teaching and learning mathematics. We recognize that this takes place within a context of national testing and statutory summative assessments by teachers, but refer the reader to other texts for these topics.

WHAT IS ASSESSED?

What is the teacher assessing? According to the usual language of externally imposed assessment, the teacher is assessing what the student knows, can do or understands, but the idea that one person can know what another knows with any precision makes no sense to us. All we can do is interpret what others do, and make inferences from our interpretations.

The student has three main ways of communicating mathematically with the teacher: orally, in writing or through some kind of physical behaviour. All of these have to be noticed and interpreted by the teacher. Even if the student communicates what appears to be correct mathematics, using conventional symbolism, the teacher cannot know whether the meanings the student is trying to convey by the symbols are the same as hers, or are going to give conventionally correct answers in other situations. For example, many students in an Australian study who said correctly that 0.05 was smaller than 0.5 were basing their answers on an idea that 0.05 was 'half of a half' and, therefore, a quarter. Some teachers, however, were taking the correct answer to be evidence of knowing about decimals.

Even more problematic is the notion of assessing 'understanding'. Taking multiplication as an example, there are many levels of understanding one might associate with it. Multiplication can mean 'lots of'; 'of' is an instruction to multiply; 'how much' is an instruction to multiply; multiplication makes things bigger; multiplication does not always make things bigger; multiplication is scaling; multiplication is about multiplication tables; multiplication can be seen as an operation on two mathematical entities and so on. All these understandings have legitimate places in the growth of mathematical knowledge and, again, the teacher cannot know precisely what the student understands at any stage. A student can be operating correctly with matrix multiplication, but still have an intuitive sense that multiplication makes things bigger. This may underly her attempts to understand matrices. This student's inability to reconcile a strongly held intuitive notion with her current work may lead her to re-examine her understanding of multiplication. Sadly, it may otherwise lead her to see mathematics as a disconnected system of rules.

These stories lead to four realizations. Firstly, that seeing how students answer questions tells us a little, but perhaps not much, about their understanding. Secondly, that it may be possible to find out more by asking more questions, and taking a variety of possible interpretations into account when teaching. Thirdly, that however much the teacher tries to identify possible meanings which students might construct, she can never be sure she has taken them all into account for her students. Lastly, all the teacher can see, hear or read is what the student *does* do, not necessarily the same as what the student *can* do or *might* do in other circumstances.

We might therefore ask what use assessment is for the teacher; what use can be made of the knowledge that a student has done three-quarters of her fraction additions correctly? The teacher would have to analyse which questions are incorrect, and find some way of seeing what features these questions have in common. It may be even more instructive to find out how the right answers were achieved to see if the methods used were generally applicable, or only worked in limited cases, such as where the denominators had no common factors so the answer cannot be simplified.

In other words, precise assessment of understanding is not possible and should not be an aim of assessment; but awareness of a possible range of understandings *is* useful for teaching purposes. Such awareness encourages teachers to devise tasks which guide students towards working on several possible conceptual understandings.

For example, imagine teaching a class about symmetries of polygons. Our past experience has shown us that some students commonly confuse 'regular' with 'symmetric'; that the diagonal of a rectangle is seen as a line of symmetry; and that a regular pentagon must look like a house, with two right angles at the base. Further discussion with individual students, triggered by asking 'how would you explain that to your younger sister or brother?' reveals some confusions. Students may be muddled about regularity because some symmetrical shapes are not irregular in the colloquial sense, only in the mathematical sense. They may believe that because the diagonal of a rectangle cuts the shape into two congruent halves it is therefore a line of symmetry. They may have never rotated a regular pentagon and seen for themselves that it is not like a house. By questioning the students in detail the teacher has uncovered the sources of confusion, and can see how the students reached their points of view. Rather than teaching them again, in a general way, the conventional approaches to these polygons, tasks can be devised which specifically focus on these erroneous beliefs. One might ask a class to draw shapes which are symmetrical but not regular and challenge them to see if there are any which are regular but not symmetric. This could lead to discussions about how to describe symmetries more precisely. One might then move on to apply these descriptions to the rectangle. Another way might be to start with the rectangle problem and ask students to draw the shapes you can make with two congruent triangles, categorize these according to reflective symmetries and so on. The teaching has been enriched by the teacher's knowledge of the students' constructions of meaning, and her understanding of how these have arisen. The tasks involve direct exploration of the sources of confusion, helping students discriminate.

If students believe that X implies Y and Y implies X, then they can be asked to create some X which are not Y, and some Y which are not X. The application of this structure to the belief that multiplication makes things bigger provides several lesson ideas. For example, students can use their calculators to find numbers which, when multiplied by 20, give a range of answers bigger *and smaller* than twenty. After a sequence of such activities they could be asked to comment on the statement 'multiplication makes things bigger' so that their new discoveries are consolidated by looking critically at their past beliefs.

KNOWING ABOUT INDIVIDUALS

In the example given above, the confusions are discovered by talking to individuals, but the tasks can be offered to the whole class as they are open-ended and could lead to a variety of other outcomes besides sorting out confusion.

How do you find out how students have constructed meaning?

Some teachers take the serious decision not to try to find out what individual students know. It is the student's business how to construe what is offered to them in mathematics lessons, and the teacher's job to create an environment in which students work mathematically with a variety of concepts, types of problem, mathematical conventions and structures. The teacher needs to take into account accumulated knowledge about the kinds of errors and confusions which arise typically in particular topics, but not necessarily relate these to individuals in the class. The underlying belief in this approach is that, by offering a variety of approaches and working on common areas of confusion, *all* learners can be helped to understand. Such teachers give support to students through teacher–student and student–student interactions, during which forms of mathematical questioning, language and symbolism are introduced and the teacher builds up a repertoire of knowledge about possible meanings the students might construct.

Others may give tests, or administer published tests, but try to find time to listen to what students say about the mistakes they make so that the teacher learns more about the sources of errors made by individual students. The teacher may then be able to adapt what is taught to take account of these, or may work with individuals to help them see things differently. It is interesting to ask students who get *right* answers to talk about the way they did their work. Many use this technique to share a variety of methods with the whole class, particularly in elementary number work, but it may be underused as an assessment tool.

Assessment activities might be devised and carried out to give information about: current understanding, accumulated knowledge, knowledge of what has recently been taught, facts, skills, techniques, communication, thinking skills, processes, speed, accuracy, learning needs, subject-specific characteristics, general intellectual character-istics, work-related characteristics, personal and social characteristics. Assessment is therefore intimately bound up with teaching, learning, classroom dynamics and a teacher's view of what knowledge of mathematics entails. For instance, if we want students to be able to discuss possible reasons behind mathematical properties, but only ever assess them on recall of facts, they will not recognize the value we put on reasoning, nor develop the skills necessary to show their reasoning in assessable forms. If we want students to be able to solve mathematical problems, but only ever assess them on 'right answer' responses, they will not recognize the value of developing thinking skills. If we want students to remember the similar properties of certain different classes of mathematical objects, but only assess exploratory work, they will not recognize the value of memory.

Through all aspects, from the way we mark books to the way we respond in lessons, and certainly the way we test them and what we do with the results, students come to know what is valued.

So how can different aspects of learning be assessed? And what sorts of planned and unplanned events happen in classrooms which inform teachers about students' knowledge? The following list of assessment strategies used by teachers is not complete, and is not in any particular order.

Assessment strategies

- setting short tasks with right answers only
- observing extended and/or open tasks, e.g. research, creative work, practical work, group work
- marking projects resulting from extended work
- encouraging oral work in class
- interviewing students
- reading and marking written work
- setting timed written work
- setting traditional tests of accumulated knowledge
- giving tests before, during, after, or some time after, a section of work
- giving annual exams
- preparing for exams (e.g. mocks)
- getting students to design tests themselves
- students assessing themselves
- having focused tests available when student requests them
- giving multiple-choice tests
- designing special assessment activities
- working on tasks and concepts which require use of a previous concept
- presenting a selected folio of illustrative work
- student explaining something to teacher
- student explaining something to another student
- hearing unexpected remarks in teacher–student conversation
- hearing a response which is unexpected, and reveals other knowledge

All the methods above are ways in which a teacher can learn more about a student's mathematics. Some of them are hard to do with a whole class because of time constraints, others are problematic because they can put some students at a disadvantage. We will not deal with problems with tests here, but instead refer the reader to *A Fair Test*, by Gipps and Murphy (1994), which describes the unfairness that can occur.

EQUITY IN ASSESSMENT

What is assessed, and how it is assessed, tells students what is considered valuable in the subject and how they can succeed in it. It is also a mechanism through which people are identified for future education or employment, particularly so in mathematics, which is a core requirement in many career paths. Whether the decisions are made by the teacher, or by an external agency such as the government, there are therefore questions about equity that need to be asked. The following list is taken largely from Gipps and Murphy:

Questions to ask about methods of testing and assessment

- How are outcomes and scores interpreted, and by whom?
- Are assessment procedures fair?
- Is the assessment relevant?
- Is the assessment useful?
- What value does the assessment have?
- What are the social consequences of assessing?
- What are the social consequences of the use of the result?
- What attention is given to marking error or bias?
- What if a test question or task is poorly constructed?
- Are there many opportunities to meet standards, or only one?
- Does everyone assessed have equal access to the same curriculum?
- Is the assessment method part of a coherent system of standards and values?
- What is the reaction of different groups to the style of assessment?
- What is the knowledge being taught?
- What is the knowledge being assessed?
- Is the assessment method appropriate for the use to which the result will be put?

Whereas these questions can obviously be applied to tests imposed from outside, and to testing procedures in school, it is less obvious that they can also be applied to teacher's own judgements made during normal classroom life. Many teachers feel that the assessments they make, based on their special knowledge of students in their regular classrooms, are much more fair than one-off assessment activities of any kind.

Think of a class you are getting to know quite well. What does 'getting to know' mean?

What information are you using to 'get to know' them?

Which aspects of that information depend on judgement, behaviour or personality?

If possible, compare your judgements to those of another teacher who teaches the same students.

Several writers have, from various perspectives, shown that teachers' decisions about their students are based largely on first impressions. If a teacher first thinks of a student as a rather good mathematician, she will be likely to interpret everything that happens afterwards from that viewpoint. Similarly, if she thinks a student is weak everything will be interpreted as if it is related to weakness. This can lead to teachers responding differently to students who are, essentially, behaving in the same way. One student who asks questions might be 'showing interest' where another one, asking similar questions, might be 'needing reassurance'. In some cases teachers can even subconsciously ignore evidence which contradicts their view, or try to explain it away as a fluke. From a perspective of justice this is a worrying finding, but awareness of the potential for bias in normal classroom judgements gives encouragement to teachers to maintain an open mind. We are not implying that teachers do this knowingly, or that their judgements are frequently wrong. However, it is important to recognize that the normal ways in which we decide how to interact with other people, and who we choose to value, apply inside the classroom as well as outside.

An increase in dependence on *mathematical* evidence, such as the quality of examples created by the student, the willingness to generalize, the kind of errors made and where they occur, the ability to spot errors and inconsistencies, rather than *social* evidence, such as willingness to take part in discussion, should also go some way towards avoiding bias.

RECOGNIZING AND WORKING WITH OUR OWN BIASES

The root problem is the basic expectation that teachers *should* be able to say something clear and summative about students' mathematics. In countries, such as the UK, where teachers are required by statute to make summative statements, a natural way forward is to work with colleagues so that decisions are made in a critical professional community rather than by individuals.

In one school we know about, teachers habitually discuss individual students and offer each other alternative interpretations of their behaviour and work. It is quite common to find two or three teachers saying things like: 'But what if the problem is that he doesn't know what division is?'; 'You may say he does not write much down, but I have found he has a lot going on in his head when I can find the time to speak with him'; 'Is his English good enough to understand the question?' This is not a suggestion that department meetings should be filled with discussions about individual students; rather, it is a suggestion that departments could regularly discuss how to improve the learning and teaching of mathematics, and the social implications of their decisions. In this particular department, teachers are going against a national trend towards ability-grouping. They are finding it ethically harder and harder to make the kind of decisions which exclude some students from certain parts of the curriculum, or which limit the possibilities for students in terms of examination entry. Their commitment to inclusion arises from professional discussion about individuals, and a team approach to developing mathematics teaching in their school.

INVOLVING STUDENTS IN ASSESSMENT

In what ways are your students able to assess their progress?

It is far more valuable for students themselves to be aware of what they are learning than for teachers to be the sole monitors of progress. For instance, asking students to explain something in their own words not only gives the teacher information, but also allows students to decide what it is they know and how to express it. Asking students to give examples is also a useful strategy. In both of these, students have to actively transform their current understanding, to reorganize it, and to decide what is relevant, what is constant and what is variable, in order to present it in a different form. Getting students to construct their own test questions is also revealing for the student, other students and the teacher. Some teachers even ask students to mark the tests as a further development of their understanding.

If the teacher is the only producer and marker of tests, and the only monitor, the view that she is the source of right answers is confirmed and some students may play the game of 'pleasing the teacher' instead of learning mathematics. Students who are given ways to take responsibility for their learning are more likely to develop understanding within an overview of the course material.

However, there is a danger that too much self-evaluation may not really trigger reflection. Repetition of form-filling can become as much an algorithmic task as arithmetical exercises can be. Words can be written with only superficial consideration to their meaning; students may write: 'I did well on this topic, it was about Z and I managed to do all the examples'.

As we have already said, students need to develop some self-awareness of their learning and most of the methods of assessment given above are still highly dependent on the teacher. Some students are naturally reflective, but others may not be so aware of their progress. We have found it helpful to ask students to spend the last few minutes of some lessons writing about what they have done during the lesson. This can take the form of creating a question or example relating to the material of the lesson. If students are involved in their own extended investigations they can also write down what they intend to do next lesson, or some unanswered questions that have occurred to them during the lesson. They can summarize what they think they have learnt, or worked towards understanding, during a lesson or sequence of lessons. Students are more likely to learn mathematics in ways which allow them to express it in recognized forms and contexts in interactive classes in which the teacher is listening, responding, questioning and prompting than in classrooms where students work largely on their own and are assessed through tests or special tasks.

Several teachers use work-in-progress boards to display ideas the students are working on, or intend to pursue next. For example, if a whole class is working on exploring linear and quadratic functions a board can be kept on which a growing number of examples can be pinned, sorted and categorized. Most primary teachers in the UK now include whole class plenary sessions at the end of each lesson, in which students compare their own results, findings and methods used during the lesson. All these strategies confirm that mathematics is more than a collection of unrelated topics and help students realize what they are learning about and how topics link together.

For more formal aspects of assessment, students can still be involved in the process by having access to the criteria used by teachers and deciding for themselves whether they can achieve these or not. Even a brief reference at the end to the aims of the lesson can trigger students to ask themselves: 'Do I understand what has been said? Have I learnt what the teacher hoped I would learn?'

SUMMARY

In this chapter we have posed questions about what the teacher can really know about students' constructions, and how this knowledge might be gained. The social justice implications for assessment, including teacher's casual judgements, have been mentioned. Several strategies for assessment have been listed, but the most useful and revealing for teachers and students appear to be those that are closely intertwined with interactive teaching.

REFERENCES

Gipps, C. and Murphy, P. (1994): *A Fair Test*. Buckingham: Open University Press.

Cooper, B. and Dunne, M. (2000): *Assessing Children's Mathematical Knowledge: Social Class, Sex and Problem-solving*. Buckingham: Open University Press.

8

Creating teaching groups

Recognition of the limitations and possibilities of working with a whole class at once, as described in the previous chapter, leads us to ask about the construction of the class. In the UK, the vast majority of mathematics classes in secondary schools are taught in groups of students who are in some way considered to have similar potential attainment in mathematics. In this chapter, setting,[1] together with the kinds of criteria used for forming teaching groups, will be examined. Arguments frequently used for setting are considered and an alternative view of teaching is developed. This alternative view arises from our practice as teachers of mixed-ability groups, but it also relates to all teaching, whether in so-called 'ability' sets or not.

What are your arguments for and against arranging students in sets according to some notion of ability? Consider the reasons used in your school for choosing to set, track or stream students.

Provide arguments in favour or against setting which you might use if your own child is placed in a lower set.

Setting means different things in different schools. Sometimes mathematics is the only subject for which students are set in this way and the constraints of timetabling may mean that they will be in their mathematics sets for other subjects as well. In one school students were taught in their mathematics sets for humanities and English. In another school, students were taught mathematics in groups which were related to whether English was their first language or not.

Being in the top set in a school with ten teaching groups is a different experience from being in the top set in a school with three groups, yet teachers frequently talk to each other about 'top set' and 'bottom set' students as if there is a common meaning. Such descriptions of groups of students are misleading and stereotyped. They also challenge the professionalism of teachers. This is particularly so with talk about 'bottom sets' as often this is related to descriptions of failure, inability, despair, bizarre behaviour and other negative characteristics of students rather than positive descriptions of potential and possibilities. In discussions with teachers about their plans for teaching lower sets the focus is often found to be on settling, calming, keeping busy, giving simple tasks or practical tasks, and relating mathematics to the outside world. Talk about top sets is more likely to be about challenge, abstraction, thinking, not being bored, being stretched and so on. We believe it is, however, desirable, possible and quite normal and sensible to speak of teaching lower sets in the same way.

A positive view of students in lower sets recognizes that, like other students, they can learn, adapt, synthesize ideas, remember facts and incidents, make choices and do a thousand and one other things. However, somewhere along the route they may have shown that there are things they cannot do, or tasks which they do not grasp as speedily as other students. A perception of lower ability, however transitory, and the decisions which follow, can have a profound effect on students for the remainder of their mathematics education.

Lower sets are often taught by less mathematically confident teachers. These teachers may have developed, through their concern for weaker students, superior skills of interaction and other techniques for motivating learners and developing independence. It could be argued that these skills are needed for all students. However, it is also common to find lower sets being offered a limited curriculum, much of which students may have met before, involving simplicity, step-by-step approaches, low-level challenges and an emphasis on keeping the class occupied and settled, rather than stimulated and actively learning.

Who is in your lower sets, and how are 'low' ability children defined?

How many students of each gender are in such sets?

How are social classes represented?

How are birthdates represented?

These questions are not frivolous. Research has shown that lower sets contain a disproportionate number of boys, of students from homes of lower socio-economic status, and of students with birthdates late in the academic year. These results force us to ask whether low achievement in mathematics is due to accidents of birth or to a complex combination of weaknesses and attitudes which are unhelpful in school and somehow exacerbated by schooling.

Since it is common to set in the UK, we have to look hard for alternative practices. We know of one school in which mathematics was taught in tutor groups, pastoral groups, mixed-ability groups until spring term of year 11 when they were regrouped according to the level of GCSE for which they were entered. Students were centrally involved in the choice of level of entry so that regrouping was not as judgmental as setting. The task of the new groups was revision and preparation for a certain known type of examination. While this arrangement was in place mathematics results in the school were higher than for any other subject apart from creative arts. Boaler (1997) compares the results of a school with similar arrangements with those of a school who taught students in sets.[2] Her findings show significantly higher achievements for weaker students and a more positive and flexible attitude to mathematics among all students in the school with mixed-ability groups.

The schools with mixed-ability mathematics teaching referred to above did not teach in ways which required, believed or expected that all students would move forward in a hierarchy of knowledge at the same testable pace. There were opportunities built into the curriculum to revisit concepts, to approach them from many different points of view, to integrate mathematical ideas into holistic projects, to focus more on mathematical thinking and mathematical behaviour rather than isolated bits of mathematical knowledge or skills, which are often the product of teaching styles dominated by textbooks or published schemes.

Research into the effects of different groupings for teaching is inconclusive, but in general it seems that setting, if it advantages anyone at all, advantages those who are already doing better than others. Mixed-ability teaching generally produces better results in external assessments for weaker students. There are also indications that different relative positions of students within a set can produce different levels of confidence and anxiety.

METHODS OF SETTING

If you teach mathematics in sets, how are your teaching groups selected?

How does this method of selection allow you to teach individuals appropriately?

There are several kinds of information which can be used to set students. The argument for setting is usually based on a need to teach individuals appropriately at some level. In the following sections we consider various methods used for deciding which students go into which sets, and ask a series of questions relating to the carefulness of the decisions. In what sense do the methods allow individuals to be taught appropriately, and in what sense might some be disadvantaged?

Setting by past achievement measured by test score

The usefulness of test results as indicators for grouping students depends to some extent on who sets the test, what it tests, and how this relates to what the teacher hopes to teach. The following could be asked:

- Does the test score tell you what you need to know to teach individuals effectively?
- How much of your planning for individuals is based on the test results?
- Is past achievement a fair predictor of future achievement?
- Do you know exactly how individual scores were achieved?
- Do you analyse what types of questions were done successfully?
- Do you analyse the kinds of errors that were made?
- Did the test refer to what had been taught to that class, or to some other standard, such as national curriculum expectations?
- Did all those who were assessed have the same kind of preparation for taking the test? For example, did they all have the same kinds of previous experience of test questions?
- Were some taught by teachers who 'taught to the test' and others taught with broader aims?
- How far does test performance reflect past teaching rather than individual potential?
- Has account be taken of well-known biases in testing methods, such as contextual questions misleading some students and aiding others, or multiple-choice questions disadvantaging some girls?

It would be an interesting experiment to offer the same students the same test a few weeks later and see how closely the results from the first test matched the results from the re-test.

Setting by particular characteristics of mathematical work

- What features are important in selecting appropriate teaching groups?
- What aspects of students' mathematical behaviour do you take into consideration?
- Does it matter if a student is good at showing working or not?
- Does it matter if one student is better with abstract questions and another with contextual questions?
- Would it make sense to have all those who prefer spatial methods in one group and those who use verbal memory, such as recall of instructions given in words, in another?

- How far are learning preferences and ways of working really individual characteristics, and how far are they reflections of past teaching?
- Is the quality of the presentation of work taken into account?

Setting by test score combined with teacher assessment

- What does teacher assessment add to the picture?
- Is the teacher's assessment based on current mathematical capability, mathematical potential, or conformity to classroom expectations?
- If the teacher's assessment differs from the test result how is this explained, and how have the assessments been standardized?
- Can the effect of teacher expectations on students' subsequent performance be taken into account?
- Are the educational aims of teaching mathematics, however they are defined, fully reflected in the aspects which the test and the teacher are jointly assessing?

Setting solely based on teacher assessment

- What safeguards are in place in case the teacher's judgement is imbalanced due to unrecognized bias, lack of evidence, over-optimism or under-estimation?
- How far does the assessment reflect the teacher's perceptions of what has been taught, and how far does it reflect what the student has actually learnt?
- Does teacher assessment reflect the educational aims of the teaching of mathematics, however they are defined?
- Is a teacher's assessment of a pupil limited to the teacher's view of mathematics, or are other views of mathematics taken into account? For example, a student who is very good at mental arithmetic, but cannot find sensible ways to record the calculations may be at a disadvantage with a teacher who insists on written methods. Can, and should, a teacher take this into account?

ALTERNATIVE PERSPECTIVES OF REASONS FOR SETTING

However carefully setting decisions are made, and whatever their basis, all result in differences within all teaching groups. If the implication is that by setting one can treat groups as if they are homogeneous in the way they learn and in the expected outcomes, then some students will be treated unfairly. Students who achieve similar test results may have arrived there by very different routes: one can be mechanistic, another deeply insightful. In contrast, students who respond to mathematics in similar ways can attain different test results.

Parental pride can exert considerable influence and power; indeed it cannot be overestimated. The fear parents have that their child will be left behind, the importance parents attach to their knowledge of where a child is in relation to others, or where they would like them to be, creates influential pressures on schools and students. It is well known that in mathematics exceptionally able children can emerge at a very young age. This impression feeds a view that a child can be damaged by being held back; the object is, therefore, to learn as much as possible as quickly as possible.

We do not intend to provide complete arguments for and against setting in this book. Instead we offer alternative views to some of the main arguments for setting. These alternatives establish a view of teaching and learning which recognizes strengths and weakness, individuality and special needs but places these in a framework of equal access to the curriculum and the development of the learner. In other words, the common belief that certain weaknesses in students translate automatically into pedagogic impossibilities is challenged.

The main arguments usually given in favour of setting are:

- mathematics is learnt in a linear fashion and students progress through the subject at a fairly steady rate;
- students learn and work in certain ways, which do not change;
- some minds are more limited than others in mathematics;
- mathematical ability is fixed and more or less the same across all areas of mathematics;
- teachers can keep track of coverage better if the range of attainment is narrow;
- setting makes it easier to motivate students appropriately;
- some teachers cannot teach brighter/weaker students;
- well-motivated students should not be distracted by less well-motivated students;
- weaker students can be given challenges only in an environment where the greater success of others is not there to demotivate.

We offer alternative ways to see each of these issues.

Mathematics is learnt in a linear fashion, students progressing through the subject at a fairly steady rate

Because some linear characteristics of mathematics seem more obvious to a lay person than, say the linear characteristics of language skills or artistic development, some people tend to assume that mathematical learning is a railway line along which each child goes, and the names of stations can be called out. Once a station has been passed there is no need to revisit it, hence there are cries of 'I've done this before' and 'you are making her do stuff she did two years ago.'

Too much attention to the main track and not enough to the view or the sidings can lead students to reach a point of confusion and being stuck. Students may have immense difficulty in relating one mathematical topic to another, or in making sense of the whole subject and their own understanding of it. It is extremely rare to find a student who is never stuck, who never has to go back and re-examine some previous knowledge, possibly from a different angle. It is far more usual for students to move forward jerkily, sometimes stuck, sometimes understanding, sometimes able to predict what is around the next bend and sometimes unable to tell you what has just been done. Sometimes there will be immense acceleration as enlightenment occurs, at other times it may be more useful to step off the track and attempt another method entirely. With this in mind, it becomes untenable to perceive that students' mathematical development is linear. It is, therefore, more sensible to create the conditions for change and for learners to have opportunities to follow a range of learning paths. Mixed-ability groups can be an environment in which such change and variability are accepted.

Students learn and work in certain ways, which do not change

The adolescent mind is not fixed, it develops as self-image, knowledge, futures and pasts are worked out through relationships with peers and adults. Setting can impose restrictions on a student's development, particularly in terms of self-image and future potential; it becomes difficult or impossible to change sets late in secondary school. Very often a change in mathematical achievement occurs because of a particular teacher and her teaching styles or increased motivation from outside the classroom, such as the prospects of a future direction or a job. Setting cannot always take the positive outcomes of such events into account.

One student missed almost a whole year of school due to a dysfunctional family in year 9 yet, because she was in a school that did not set students, ended up with a grade B in mathematics at the end of year 11. Another student who had been disruptive, often excluded, and had no work to show for years 9 and 10, (in fact he had done so little that no one had any idea of his mathematical potential, only of his apparent lack of social potential) became remotivated in the spring term of year 11; because he was in a mixed-ability environment, was able to pick up and respond to the high expectations amongst other students in the group. Instead of the predicted grade F he got a C.

In contrast, a student in a second set gained much higher marks in a national test than several in the top set, yet the school was unable to move her to the top set because she had missed some of the syllabus.

Some minds are more limited than others

Setting suggests that there are limitations on the power of the human mind in its capability to learn and construct its own patterns and meanings. It is clear, from psychological theory and from observing people in non-school contexts, that every brain has this capability, even those assigned to bottom sets. In fact, one of the features of bottom set classes is the extraordinary range of unusual and unhelpful constructions of mathematical understanding, coupled with a patchy sense of pattern and meaning in mathematics often due to poor school attendance! How can teachers be sure that their ideas about learning are correct, definite and secure enough that students are being properly treated by setting? Is it possible that students' potential is being mistreated by setting?

One of the authors recently taught a bottom set year 9 in an inner-city school for two lessons a week in order to find out if abstract ways of working on mathematics, such as those Krutetskii (1976) suggested were typical of gifted students, were possible to achieve with weaker students. In the space of one term, nearly all students had shown they were able to work, at least some of the time, at the higher, complex, more abstract levels he describes. For example, one student was asked to plot points using some given coordinate pairs and join them up to form a picture. She reported finding this boring and, instead, examined the sequence of pairs to identify and classify the lines she would eventually have to draw. This done, she drew in all the lines of a certain length and gradient, then all the lines of another length and gradient, and so on. She lacked the language of gradient or vectors, but she had, in effect, developed the concept of vector for herself to make the work more interesting.

Mathematical ability is more or less the same across all areas of mathematics

Some students are excellent at working with shape and space but weak on number. Others have different strengths and weaknesses. It is false to try and force everyone through each aspect of the curriculum at the same pace or to judge them as if they should be making uniform progression. A student who needs extra help with spatial work may be very sophisticated with algebraic and abstract skills. By contrast there are excellent mathematicians who find arithmetic fraught with insecurity. Krutetskii (1976) points out that accuracy in calculation is not a necessary characteristic of gifted mathematicians! Setting can restrict, or fail to acknowledge, differences in learning outcomes and imposes a false evenness onto the student's mathematics which can mask potential achievement because some aspects of mathematics are untaught or unassessed.

Teachers can keep track of coverage better if the range of attainment is narrow

It is usually difficult to cater for everyone in the room if there is a wide range of attainment and, therefore, much easier if everyone is assumed to be of a similar ability. However, it becomes much easier if one plans lessons in terms of exploring topic areas and providing mathematically fruitful activities (such as those we offer in this book) rather than in terms of covering topics or completing a chapter in a textbook or a set of exercises. In fact it can be dangerous to plan according to expected coverage because, however carefully you do this, you cannot assume or know how much different students have remembered or understood as a result of engaging with previous topics. It is by understanding mathematics that our knowledge grows. If students simply 'do' topics they do not necessarily become more able to learn mathematics for themselves.

Teachers may attempt to aim coverage at a notional middle of the group but the assumption that all students come with the same knowledge, learn the same way, listen with the same attention and construct the same picture, is false. The provision of activities which lead to clearly perceived, differentiated, outcomes from which we can see what mathematics has been done, used and understood, allows the monitoring of learning (as far as we can tell anything about someone else's learning). As a consequence, assessments of students' mathematical attainment can be based on what they have shown they know and can do, rather than on coverage. By 'shown' we mean through a variety of ways by which students might communicate mathematics, verbally, in written and diagrammatic forms and practically.

Setting makes it easier to motivate students appropriately

Setting may lead to false expectations, both of teacher and student. Students in top sets can become complacent because they have, at some time, been labelled as 'good' and 'successful'. Furthermore, those students who are placed in a top set but struggle to keep up with the pace of delivery are likely to gain a sense that they are failing to meet the teacher's expectations.

All students should have enough to challenge them in whichever way they are grouped. This may not be achieved by limiting the school curriculum to the examination syllabus and certain predictable examination question types. Students in lower sets might be discouraged, or offered a limited diet. One cannot be sure that equality of opportunity is being offered to all students, particularly if different curricula are being given to different groups of students. Teachers can look for ways to introduce topics, which are defined as 'hard' by historical expectations, to students whose achievements appear to be lower in national curriculum terms. Skilful teachers have always worked on ways to make the difficult more accessible.

Sometimes it is in tackling something hard that students finally come to understand something thought of as easier. An example of how working in a complex situation can enlighten students about simpler situations is the process of turning fractions into decimal fractions. Exploration of recurrence provides a context for revising division algorithms; more than this, it provides a context for developing understanding of division by encouraging students to look at the remainders they are getting, examine cycles of recurrence, and so on. (Further examples of difficult topics are developed in Chapters 9 to 14.)

When thinking about motivation, therefore, a key issue is *what* it is possible to motivate students to do, rather than *how* to motivate them to do something simple, or something which limits or underestimates their potential. The relationship between self-motivation and success in students is complex; one aspect does not clearly precede another. If higher sets are better motivated, this could be either an effect or a cause of being in a high set. It might also point to the effects of having challenging expectations, which students are then helped to attain.

Some teachers cannot teach brighter/weaker students

All teachers occasionally find themselves teaching students who are 'brighter' than they themselves were. Some teachers are puzzled about how to teach those who repeatedly fail to understand mathematics in conventional ways. They cope not by pretending or wishing they were 'brighter' themselves but by developing the craft of teaching and working on how to enable such students to access higher level thinking and extend their mathematics. A teacher is an expert in planning, designing and assessing learning and a partial expert in subject knowledge. A good teacher can provide questions, prompts, materials, ideas and resources for any student rather than trying to transmit knowledge or leaving the student to work through an advanced textbook alone. In fact, if the concentration of effort is placed upon the *processes* of mathematical work, rather than the content, students will be able to pursue any questions or suggestions. They can also be encouraged to raise queries by using investigative skills and engaging with suitably challenging starting points. Reliance on a transmission of knowledge model restricts the way a teacher can teach, who they can teach and who will understand it.

A teacher who, in spite of her craft knowledge, still lacks confidence can be supported by a team. We would say that all teachers work better in teams in which ideas about how to tackle particular topics can be shared and bounced around. Perhaps team teaching is a good way to use the strengths of two teachers and enable each to develop in their areas of weakness. Another useful support strategy, which is, unfortunately, rarely possible to organize, is to try to arrange opportunities for colleagues to observe each other and offer comments on lessons. Such peer-evaluation can make a valuable addition to personal and departmental development. This strategy can also be used for teachers who do not feel they have the right skills to teach weaker students, or those with special educational needs. A further strategy is for a pair of teachers to plan jointly and agree to provide the same starting points to their classes. Discussion after lessons about what transpired, what similar and different outcomes occurred, what went well, and what needs to be tweaked and refined can lead to constructive and supportive, shared professional development.

Well-motivated students should not be distracted by less well-motivated students

It is sometimes said that well-motivated students have to be allowed to get on with their work, and not be held back by slower or noisier workers. Achievement and motivation are not necessarily correlated. High achieving school students can be lazy and restrict themselves to minimal requirements, such as what is necessary for examinations. Some lower achieving students are very hard workers. If, however, it does turn out to be the case that those in lower sets are least motivated there is always the question of whether this is cause or effect. Whatever the teacher's theory, it becomes a responsibility to allow *all* students to get on with their work, and encourage all to develop concentration and determination. It is easier to do this in a class which contains a mixture of role-models than in one where only similar behaviour is seen. How can students with low motivation learn that other behaviour is possible except by seeing peers behaving differently?

The teacher's role is to make sure the work is appealing and worth doing and also help students to overcome their own weaknesses and negativity, which lead to poor motivation. Negotiation over rules for acceptable behaviour in the classroom helps here. Very often, if the expectations and agreements are clear, those who cannot sustain the effort turn out to be those who have a range of other difficulties working against them too. This does not always mean the same as low ability. In fact, the student might be inarticulately aching for an appropriate challenge through which she can earn some self-esteem.

Good teachers know that helping students overcome poor motivation is their responsibility just as much as any other aspect of a student's underachievement. We conjecture that it is easier to involve all students in a class where there is a mixture of all kinds of motivation than in one in which there are many poor role models.

Weaker students can be given challenges only in an environment where the greater success of others is not there to demotivate

It is sometimes said that weaker students can only be given challenges and the opportunity for success if they are not in an environment where everyone else is doing better than they are. The success of others might be a disincentive if they know they could never achieve similar outcomes however hard they try. In our experience, however, we have many 'weaker' students who have provided valuable contributions in classes and offered positive role models of effort and achievement to others.

Several mathematics teachers have personal experience of this, having, at some point in their school careers, found themselves struggling with mathematics alongside students for whom it seems much easier. Their response was usually to develop learning skills, and insights into the structures of meaning in mathematics, to internalize mathematics in a way that those who grasped methods and techniques easily did not always do. Stories of students who gained easy A grades at school but dropped out of university courses abound, but there are complementary stories of students who went on to graduate well in mathematics having appeared relatively weak at school.

With a highly heterogeneous mix of students there is a wide experience of learning to exploit, and many opportunities to learn the value of giving and accepting support for one's learning. Rather than this being seen as 'helping the others' or 'waiting for others to catch up' it can be seen as an opportunity to transform one's existing knowledge into a form that is accessible to someone else, and hence a process of consolidation and search for depth. Furthermore, in many countries, it is seen culturally as an educational responsibility all students have to the whole community to help others understand what they themselves already understand.

What is important for all students is to be challenged to compete with their own previous work; this is very different from competing with a notional class performance, or a set of externally written standards of attainment.

A FURTHER LOOK AT SETTING

Try to list the students in a mathematics class in order of achievement.

What criteria are you using? What difficulties or issues arise?

How might you annotate or modify your list so another teacher can use it?

What does the list tell you? What does the list predict about students?

Setting is often based on summative information from previous schools, entry tests or standardized records. The first type of information depends on another teachers' judgements relating to the past and to particular styles of teaching. They do not necessarily predict the future except in a self-fulfilling, prophetic way.

Tests show a partial picture of knowledge, show no picture of current or future learning and may contain questions which are ambiguous, impenetrable or emotive. In addition test answers may conceal knowledge where the child has misunderstood the question. For instance:

Question: *Even numbers are those which have 2 as a factor. List even numbers up to 10.*
Darren's answer: *3, 6, 9*

In this example, it is clear that Darren knows something, possibly about factors, possibly about evenly-spaced numbers up to ten. He appears to have misunderstood the question. The written answer on its own does not tell us whether he can or cannot understand even numbers.

Records may be based on teacher assessment, or coverage, or progress through a published scheme. All of these may be closely related to teachers' expectations and interpretations rather than the students' understanding. If the information comes from a school which already sets students then their progress will have already been affected by the setting decisions and treatment. Again, it does not tell you much about what future progress might be in a different environment.

What, for instance, happens to the student who has been allowed to spend time exploring lots of ideas about shape, is the class expert on icosahedra but whose data-handling is relatively weak because she was finishing her shape project while the others were doing a survey? Should she be 'above' because of her skills in using and applying mathematics, her self-motivation and evident interest in the subject, or should she be 'below' because she does not have as much curriculum coverage as some others? A common response to such conundrums is to prevent students from pursuing project work for too long so that curriculum coverage can be accounted for. This message contradicts good practice with respect to motivation, interest and understanding. A different response is to argue that the development of mathematical thinking, mathematical understanding and self-esteem arising from extended work enables students to learn better in the long run by enabling them to construct their own complex networks of mathematics to which future topics can be related. However, this attitude is hard to express convincingly in a system involving frequent content-based tests.

SOCIAL CLASS

Whatever methods of setting are used, a relationship between social class and setting hierarchies is liable to develop. Those selected for top sets might have been chosen according to their knowledge of how classrooms work. Those who know most tend to be from middle-class families whose parents had post-compulsory education themselves. Those who had nursery education, or knowledgable and supportive parenting at home, or were surrounded by books or adult conversation, or were offered a variety of experiences of travel, theatre, museums, hobbies, music, and so on invariably end up better equipped to use school to their own best advantage. These children show classroom superiority from the beginning, being able to talk, listen, accept that effort brings results and understand the need for organization and structure. The highest group is most likely to contain middle-class children because it is, in effect, selected not on the basis of potential, for that is very hard to measure, but on attainment, school behaviour and motivation, which might reflect class and background.

> *... homogeneous forms of grouping reinforce segregation of pupils in terms of social class ...* (Sukhnandan & Lee, 1998)[3]

We are not saying that these children should *not* have the high expectations and challenges that being in the top set might bring, or that they do not deserve them. They should have them, do deserve them and will be able to use them. What we are saying is that *all* children deserve these attitudes to be affecting their work, and *all* children could use them. We never accepted it as part of our job to decide in advance what each child can do in the future, but to try our best to find ways of teaching that enable as many children as possible to understand and progress in the present.

Setting might deny access to the whole of mathematics because teachers can talk themselves into believing that some students can or cannot be expected to learn certain things. In groups in which mathematics on several different levels is going on, students can see and be attracted by all sorts of mathematics without being hampered by the notion of 'level'. To give an example, we have, for many years, decided to teach trigonometry to whole mixed-ability classes. It is not necessary to decide in advance who will or will not be able to understand trigonometry. Given an appropriate starting place to construct meanings for trigonometry, all students can engage with trigonometric and related ideas (see chapter 9).

DISADVANTAGES OF MIXED-ABILITY TEACHING

A question which could, and should, be asked of every educational decision is: 'Who will be advantaged, and who disadvantaged, by this decision?' In the interests of equity we should, therefore, also discuss the negative effects of mixed-ability teaching. It is true of any teaching arrangements that they only succeed if they are skillfully and professionally used. The kinds of classroom we describe require energetic, committed teachers who are confident in their inclusive work with adolescents or their inclusive work with mathematics, and preferably both. In our experience having one kind of confidence can be enough at the start; the other grows with reflective practice and support.

Teaching and learning that depend on reproduction of technical skills cannot be generally successful in mixed-ability classes, as it cannot take into account different qualities of prior knowledge, different understandings of concepts and different ways of learning. There will always be some who struggle, get nowhere, and eventually give up. Similarly, teaching that attempts merely to prepare students for future tests cannot be successful, particularly if different tests are to be taken for different expected levels of achievement. A curriculum plan that requires topics to be covered explicitly may be inappropriate for mixed-ability teaching because it does not allow for the different mathematical interests, needs and strengths.

The kind of topic-centred curriculum and testing regime now extant in UK schools has led to increased setting, even in primary schools, because teachers cannot see ways to teach that 'cover' the curriculum and prepare students for tests. If the educational aim of teaching mathematics is to fit all students into a given curriculum, a given order of learning and a rigorous testing regime, then clearly there will be insuperable difficulties: most students will not fit! Although we think this book contains many ways to work with all abilities within the current framework we also recognize setting as a pragmatic response to such expectations. In some cases setting is used in order to ensure that the higher achieving students have teachers with more mathematical knowledge, and the other adults available can be focused on classes of lower achievers, which often contain smaller numbers. In this sense one could argue that setting is *more* equitable in that it provides the different kinds of knowledgeable teaching required by students with different educational needs and, moreover, that students can only compare themselves to others whose achievements are realistically related to their own. In mixed-ability arrangements, all teachers have to provide appropriate challenge and support for all kinds of student, and all students have a full range of achievement with which to compare themselves.

INCLUSIVITY

Setting can be based on judgements about motivation and the limitations of certain teaching methods. These can be seen instead as challenges to the craft of teaching and not as reasons to set. We would go further than this and say that setting might be a response to the belief that difference is a *problem* rather than a natural human characteristic. It is strange that, at a time when differences of race, gender, class and physical ability are being actively incorporated into inclusive classrooms, with all the associated challenges and rewards, that grouping by judgements of past progress is common in mathematics teaching, and even encouraged by governments.

How often are the principles and methods of grouping in your department reviewed?

For us, inclusivity can only be achieved by the development of teaching methods that allow for all students to have access to the same range of mathematics, accept different outcomes, offer several opportunities to develop understanding of key ideas and demonstrate a clear belief and commitment to changing expectations of teachers and learners.

SUMMARY

In this chapter we have raised questions about the growing orthodoxy of placing students in setted groups to learn mathematics. We have explored the implications of creating stereotyped expectations, of providing different curricular to different groups, of what being in a 'top' or a 'bottom' set means and the effects this can have upon students' confidence and self-perception.

We have examined methods used to determine how individuals are selected for certain sets, and raised concerns over the accuracy and the validity of such methods.

We have countered the usual arguments offered in support of setting, and described ways of working with students of wide-ranging abilities. The impact this has upon lesson planning and for curriculum and personal development was also explored. (We refer the reader to Sukhnandan and Lee (1998) for more information).

The rest of this book gives much practical advice for teaching any mathematics group, but all of it applies equally well to inclusive groups and mixed-ability groups of any kind.

NOTES

1. This word is used in UK to describe the separation of students into teaching groups for mathematics which are based on some notion of students' mathematical ability. Students are not necessarily with the same groups for their other lessons.
2. She matches the schools for other factors such as social and geographical context.
3. The use of 'homogeneous' here is misleading. Any set will be heterogeneous in terms of knowledge, memory, learning styles and affective factors.

REFERENCES

Boaler, J. (details at the end of chapter 1)

Sukhnandan, L. and Lee, B. (1998) *Streaming, Setting and Grouping by Ability : a Review of the Literature* (Slough: NFER). The authors collect a wide range of research results comparing the effects of different kinds of grouping on attainment. The overall message is mixed, and research design is an important factor in the results, but in general it is found that average and below average students do better in mixed-ability groupings while the very brightest might do less well.

Krutetskii, V. A. (1976) (trans. J.Teller) in J. Kilpatrick and I. Wirszup (eds) *The Psychology of Mathematical Abilities in School Children* (Chicago: University of Chicago Press). This is a detailed study of the ways of thinking and working with mathematics which gifted mathematics students appear to use.

Part Two
Mathematics for all

In the following chapters we focus on some typical mathematical content areas and show how our planning to teach incorporates inclusivity, access and equality of opportunity.

A sense of hierarchy within mathematics can lead to the belief that learners must be able to do simple aspects of mathematics before they can understand more complex ideas. The complexity of trigonometry sometimes leads to the belief that it is an unsuitable topic for weaker students to be taught. Our view is that *all* students benefit from engaging with complex mathematics. It is the teacher's job to find ways to approach complex ideas that intrigue students, to encourage them to grapple with the simpler components of the work, to look for analogies, metaphors and demonstrations that promote access to the topic, to use different ways of seeing the topic. One way to do this is to identify the simpler components, and how they combine with each other, and then to think of ways in which students can do this for themselves. Other ways are shown in context in the next six chapters, in which we give a selective treatment of some aspects of the secondary mathematics curriculum to illustrate how our approach might be used to teach core topics.

Most students are capable of engaging in some way with the whole of the school curriculum. Engagement is sometimes naive, mechanical, sometimes based on idiosyncratic interpretation, but frequently complex and imbued with meaning.

How can complex concepts be made accessible so you do not need, beforehand, to make decisions about who may or may not understand something?

> *All I must do is to present them (the students) with a situation so elementary that they all master it from the outset, and so fertile that they will all find a great deal to get out of it.* (Gattegno; 1963, p. 63).

Finding accessible places to start, from which all students can construct an understanding of desired concepts, is an essence of planning. Other elements are: inclusion of all students, differentiated learning outcomes, using problem-solving approaches where possible and appropriate, allowing students to construct and reconstruct meaning from a variety of experiences, getting students to set up and solve their own and each others' problems, using practical, verbal, symbolic and image-based approaches where possible and appropriate, and giving students choices about the work they do.

Each chapter concludes with a summary of strategies that can be used in many contexts.

9

Trigonometry

The first concept we have chosen to use to illustrate an approach to teaching is trigonometry. Consider the following questions:

What do you consider to be the key, basic mathematical ideas that students will need to know before they understand sine and cosine?

Suppose that 'understanding sine and cosine' appeared in your scheme of work two years earlier than it does at present. How would you plan to teach this? What changes would you make to the way you currently teach it?

What situations might you set up which are elementary but fertile?

POSSIBLE APPROACHES TO TEACHING SINE AND COSINE

In planning to teach trigonometry, one possible starting point is to ask students to consider the free end of a rotating ray of fixed length and recognize that the locus traced is a circle. Students are then asked to explore what happens to the position of the point by reading coordinates for different degrees of turn. Thus practice of use of coordinates is incorporated into exploration of another topic; one *has* to use the conventional notation to be included in what the rest of the class does.

We have used five different ways to begin:
- The teacher describes the rotating arm using a diagram on a square-grid blackboard; or the teacher silently produces the diagram and asks students what they observe.
- Using an OHT with a square grid and part of a protractor transposed onto the grid, the teacher or a student demonstrates the rotating arm.
- Students are given a set of instructions about how to make their own rotating arm; in this case the teacher prompts students to think about the mathematics instead of staying at a practical level. For example, students can be asked to predict the locus of the end of the arm, or to notice any grid points through which it will pass.

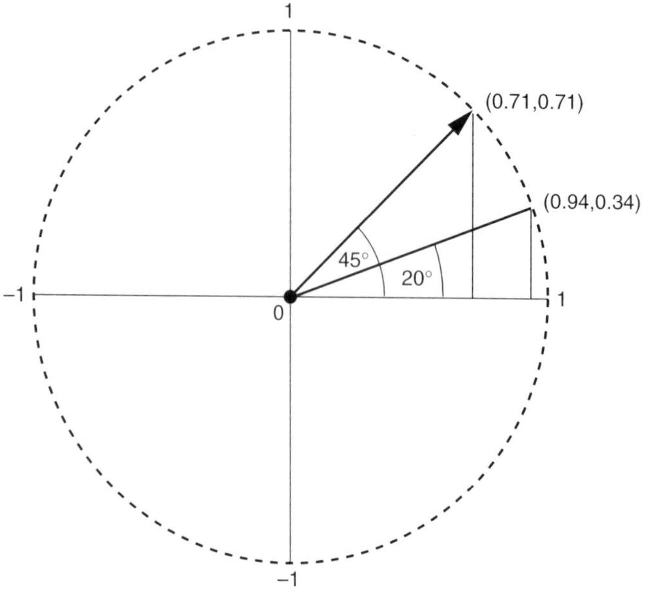

Fig. 7.

- The teacher prepares a procedure using dynamic geometry software and students use this to gather information (the *x* and *y*-ordinates); here the teacher has to prompt students to think mathematically within the software environment, rather than focusing on features of the software.
- Students are asked to imagine a circle with a point moving around the circumference. Often we ask them to describe to their neighbours what they see.

There are three basic ideas that students will need to recall: how to read the coordinates of points on a grid, that a scale from 0 to 1 can be split up into ten equal sections as 0.1, 0.2 ... and that angle is a measure of turn. However, we would not call these 'prerequisites' if that is taken to mean that students who cannot recall them should be excluded from the activity. The work can be preceded by a discussion in which these ideas are reviewed. Other adults, such as LSAs, can be briefed about these and encouraged not to let weaker students get trapped in the elementary aspects of the work. The adults could be doing these simpler things so that the student can be concentrating on the implications of the results.

Students then read off the coordinates of the end point of the rotating arm, of length 1, for angles from $0°$ to $90°$ in $10°$ turns. Using

1 mm or 2 mm graph paper, it is possible to record answers to two decimal places. Having completed this task, there are a number of possible developments: to look at the results achieved and make comments about what they observe; to consider when the x-ordinate and the y-ordinate are equal; to estimate some intermediate readings; to estimate what the angle would be for given x and y-ordinates; to estimate x and y-ordinates for angles $> 90°$; to draw graphs to connect angle with x-ordinates and y-ordinates; to reverse the earlier process and calculate what angle would be if the y ordinate was, say, 0.6. Each of these tasks can lead to further explorations, for example, when students have drawn the two graphs they can be asked to consider simultaneous solutions.

Some of these tasks are appropriate for whole class discussion, for students to report back to everyone what they have found, to be set for homework, or to be displayed as work-in-progress. Others are more appropriate for the teacher to suggest to students as they are working, offering different questions to different students or groups of students.

Up to this point students have been reading off coordinate values, to two decimal places, for a set of points which happen to trace out a circle. The next task could be to compare the angle values previously gathered with results gained by keying 'cos' and 'sin' on a calculator for each of these angles. The intention here is for students to recognize that the results from the coordinate diagram are similar to those now gained from the calculator. This can be done with the whole class and students can be asked by name to say what they find. All students can thus be included, even if they cannot all immediately see the similarities between the values. Furthermore there is an opportunity in this context for students to round off their calculator results to two decimal places. For some students this will be relatively straightforward, whereas for others this will be an opportunity to practise the skill, possibly after receiving some 'direct' input from the teacher or another student about how to do so.

Having compared and connected the two sets of results, students can construct an image on which to base their understanding of the terminology of cosine and sine, i.e. the horizontal and vertical readings of the coordinates of the end point of an arm, of length 1, as it rotates in a circle. The use of trigonometry in the context of angles in triangles is a part of this larger picture. Of course some students may only appreciate the equalities at a naive level at this stage. They may not be surprised or appreciate the significance of their findings unless the classroom ethos is of discovery, conjecture and pleasure in making connections in mathematics.

Being explicit about what has been done and learnt

At some point in all this doing it is important for students to take stock of what they have learnt. There are two ways students might achieve this. One is for them to write about what they have understood, what they have observed and what connections they have made. Another is for students to talk about what they have understood. It is unrealistic to expect the teacher to find time to listen to all the students; for this reason it is important that students learn how to write about, or otherwise record on paper, their mathematics. Such writing can include diagrams and examples. Expecting students to record what they have been doing, in order to make sense of it, is an important part of helping students deepen their understanding.

In this activity they could include: when the horizontal reading of one result is the same as the vertical reading for another result and recognizing how each pair of angles always adds up to 90; when the horizontal reading, or x-ordinate, is the same as the cosine reading; how their initial results compare with the calculator readings; the significance of angles such as $30°$ and $60°$, $45°$ ($135°$, $225°$ etc.); comments on the shapes of the graphs; comments about where the graphs cross, when they become negative, what happens after $360°$ and so on.

The language of trigonometry

The next stage could be to develop the idea of what happens to horizontal and vertical readings as the arm length changes from 1 to (say) 2, 3, 2.5, 2.7 and so on. This enlargement process is a development from the starting point. Students often produce a calculator procedure; this needs to be connected with the original situation and translated explicitly into the language of right angled triangles, that is, the hypotenuse, and opposite and adjacent sides to a given angle. Helping students get to grips with such vocabulary is essential and using a more didactic style, using the language publicly, contrasts with the more investigative approach adopted earlier. Explicit use of language by the teacher and the insistence that students also use such technical language in a whole class setting enhances this juxtaposition of investigative and didactic approaches to learning. Exploration has aroused intrigue and interest; discussion has allowed images of concepts to be developed; finally these concepts are labelled in a conventional, agreed manner.

Student-generated problems

To help students become familiar with this vocabulary and confident in its use they can set up and solve their own or each other's problems.

Each draws a right-angled triangle and then measures an angle and the length of the hypotenuse. They use sine and cosine to calculate the lengths of the opposite and adjacent sides. Using a ruler, the two sides are measured and compared with the calculations. They do this enough times to convince themselves they have an understanding of the processes involved; they can also draw right-angled triangles which are not orientated in the usual ways, (i.e. with sides parallel to the edges of the paper), thereby forcing themselves to decide which sides are opposite or adjacent to the given angle.

Students can be set further tasks to devise procedures that calculate the unknown angles and the hypotenuse for other right-angled triangles. By working from 'real' information, actual triangles drawn by themselves, setting and solving their own problems, the process becomes self-checking. At each stage it is important to develop recording skills by encouraging students to show what calculator sequences they have used when working out the desired information.

Further extension tasks

Of course some students will be ready to advance well beyond this level and appreciate sine and cosine as functions. One extension task could be to consider what happens to graphs of functions such as $f(x) = 2\sin x$, or $f(x) = \sin 2x$ and so on. Providing students with a photocopy of their earlier graph of $f(x) = \sin x$, allows them to superimpose these other graphs and to make comparisons and generalizations.

Another extension is to use the rotating arm image to provide a 'gateway' for students to make sense of the formula $\sin^2 x + \cos^2 x = 1$ and connect it to Pythagoras' theorem. Indeed one of us, whilst working with final year mathematics undergraduates, witnessed students' expression of considerable surprise when this connection was so clearly demonstrated and explicitly recognized.

TANGENTS

The tangent of an angle can be seen as a development of the rotating point, but here we treat this notion directly. The vocabulary of sides 'opposite' and 'adjacent to' a given angle requires a careful explanation. Students are asked to gather some information, individually in the first instance, by drawing a number of right-angled triangles on 1 cm squared grid paper, and carrying out some measures and calculations. The table below is an example of information collected from four possible triangles. When students are asked to record results in a table, some take a long time drawing the lines and focusing on neatness instead of mathematics. This can be avoided by providing pre-printed tables.

Students would need to collect several more such sets of information, in order to be in a position to analyse connections between the angle and the ratios $o:a$ and $a:o$.

opposite length	adjacent length	Measured angle	$o:a$ as a fraction	$o:a$ as a decimal
5	2	68	5/2	2.5
1	3	18	1/3	0.333
3	4	37	3/4	0.75
3	2	56	3/2	1.5

Once students have collected several pieces of information they can compare their results and collect their information together. A spreadsheet can be very useful. A discussion about how to organize the results in some sort of order is also useful.

When students compare results, some will have the same or equivalent information. For instance, one triangle with $o = 2$ and $a = 3$ will have the same angle and decimal ratio as a triangle with $o = 4$ and $a = 6$.

They respond in writing to questions such as:

What happens to the ratio between the two 'short' sides as the angle increases?

What happens to the angle as the ratio increases?

What is special about those angles where the ratio is 1?

What does the graph of angle plotted against the decimal ratio look like?

What is the connection between information gathered for tangents and the coordinate pairs gathered in the work on sine and cosine?

These questions can be posed to the whole class, or to individuals and groups, or displayed on a poster for students to choose what they do next.

Having established some of these connections a new task could be to measure two of the 'short' sides and calculate the angle, or measure one side and the angle and determine the other short side. This can be done using a calculator, or by estimating from information already collected. Again students can do as many of these as they need to and check their answers. In this way students explore given situations and also have some control over the type and amount of information gathered. There is no need to use an exercise from a worksheet or a textbook because the activities generate practice themselves.

Tangent can also be seen by extending the rotating-arm radius until it intersects with a vertical tangent drawn to the circle where it meets the horizontal axis. The vertical height of the intersection gives the tangent. A colleague suggested drawing the tangent to the circle at the end of the radius, then the length along it from the circle to the horizontal axis gives the tangent. These approaches can also be included in the use of dynamic geometry software mentioned earlier. There are, of course, other ways that concepts of sine, cosine and tangent can be taught. The above descriptions are not intended to be prescriptions. Indeed a central part of our professional development as teachers has involved adopting and adapting ideas from a variety of sources and contexts; little is new and much is borrowed and shaped.

STRATEGIES USED IN THIS CHAPTER

- offering a visual image on chalkboard, OHP, or computer screen, either silently or with explanation, operated by teacher or students;
- asking students what they think might happen in a dynamic situation;
- asking students to imagine a geometric situation;
- using skills developed previously;
- asking students to say what they observe about some numerical results or shapes of graphs;
- asking students to talk in pairs about what they see;
- intervening during practical or computing tasks with questions which focus on mathematics;
- using graphs to estimate in order to work with relationships;
- incorporating skills such as rounding and estimation in other curriculum tasks;
- incorporating repeated calculations and skills within tasks to provide practice;
- avoiding letting weaker students get 'bogged down' in elementary aspects of the work;
- working with supporting adults on how to help weaker students get to the main focus of the lesson, possibly by removing obstacles due to poor memory or technique;
- introducing trigonometry functions as a way to describe a phenomenon;
- using calculators to compare function values with values generated another way;
- choosing which tasks to give to a whole class, which to discuss with a whole class, and which are better for individuals or small groups;

- asking students to write about their work;
- providing ways to record work which discourage spending too long a time on neatness;
- displaying work in progress;
- asking students to talk about what they understand;
- include all students in discussion by encouraging contributions, possibly prepared beforehand;
- extending the work to explore more complicated trigonometric functions;
- having a variety of questions and extensions available, possibly displayed somewhere;
- linking to other mathematical topics, providing an element of surprise;
- using and practice of technical vocabulary;
- asking students to set problems for each other;
- giving students a model of how to explore an area of mathematics and let them re-use these methods in a slightly different context;
- aiming for all students to have a useful image of a concept to which they can refer in future.

REFERENCES

Beeney, R. *et al.* (1982) *Geometric Images.* Derby: Association of Teachers of Mathematics.

Gattegno, C. (1963) *For the Teaching of Mathematics (Volume 1).* Reading: Educational Explorers.

10

Aspects of shape

In this chapter we work with shapes by exploring moves made on a coordinate grid and a variety other grids based upon the 30°, 60°, 90° triangle, the 45°, 45°, 90° triangle, and others.

It is by moving shapes around that students come to be aware of what stays the same and what changes. Working on variance and invariance is a fundamental teaching and learning activity. There is a crucial difference, at school mathematics level, between reflecting a shape successively in several lines, such as one might do when tessellating, and considering reflections as actions on the *plane*, rather than the shape. In some activities students typically handle cutouts of shapes, flip them and replace them on the paper and talk of reflecting shapes. In others, the student has to imagine the whole plane and everything on it being reflected, but may retain the language and mental imagery of handling the shapes. For this reason we refer to 'flips' where the mirror lines take several positions and have kept the word 'reflection' for reflective transformations that might be expressed as simple matrices.

TRANSFORMATIONS ON A COORDINATE GRID

A simple, accessible, starting point is for students to observe what happens to a shape as the coordinates that define the corners of the shape change according to different rules.

Students draw an asymmetric quadrilateral with corners defined by, for example: **A** (2,1); **B** (2,3); **C** (4,3); and **D** (5,1), and then apply some changes to the (x,y) coordinates of the vertices of the shape. In the table below we suggest some possible changes. In the second column we give some concepts with which students will work as a result of particular prompts:

What happens to the orientation and area of the shape ABCD when you:	Concepts under consideration
Add 1 to each ordinate?	Vector shift. Area conserved.
Double each ordinate?	Enlargement by scale factor (SF) × 2, centre (0,0). Area enlarged 4 times.
Halve each ordinate?	Enlargement by SF × 0.5, centre (0, 0). Area enlarged by SF × 0.25.
Swap the ordinates around? (or mis-plot the coordinates!)	Reflection in $y = x$.
Make the x-ordinate negative?	Reflection $x = 0$.
Make the y-ordinate negative?	Reflection $y = 0$.
Make both ordinates negative?	Double reflection in axes, or rotation through 180° about centre (0,0).
Make both ordinates negative then double each one?	Double reflection, or rotation of 180°, followed by enlargement SF × 2, or enlargement SF × −2 from the origin.
Make each ordinate negative and swap them over?	Reflection in $y = -x$.
Multiply each ordinate by two then add one to each result?	Enlargement SF × −2 from centre (−1,−1).
Multiply the x-ordinate by 2 and keep the y-ordinate the same?	Skew

As in the previous chapter, teachers choose which tasks are for the whole class, which can be directed at individuals or small groups, or whether students can choose for themselves what they pursue. Students who have difficulty with drawing can give instructions to other students, or to supporting adults, or use software to produce diagrams rather than be excluded from the main focus of the lesson. They can then concentrate on making observations, predictions and generalizations from the diagrams alongside the other students.

DIFFERENTIATION THROUGH GIVING STUDENTS MORE RESPONSBILITY

Because students can create their own directions of investigation by using similar questions, they can take increased responsibility for the work they do. An obvious and useful way to hand over responsibility is to ask students to produce their own shapes, slightly more complex than a square, and repeat the explorations. Responsibility for problem-posing need not rest with the teacher, other adults, or a textbook, but students need experiences within which problem-posing arises naturally from their investigations in order to develop a propensity to pose mathematical problems in *any* mathematical activity.

A potential power of this approach is that the same questions can be posed to classes of all ages and levels of attainment. Whilst younger students might focus more on plotting coordinates in four quadrants and recognizing the types of transformations that occur, older students can be expected to justify *why* the underlying geometric results occur, and perhaps prove this. Furthermore, the same questions could be used as an entry point to teach transformations by matrices.

Differentiation is taken into account by providing a set of simple starting points to give access to a range of 'basic' concepts, while the same starting points can be used to lead other students towards understanding deeper, much more complex ideas and mathematical structures.

CONTEXTS FOR PRACTISING A RANGE OF SKILLS AND DEVELOPING SPATIAL ARGUMENTS

Students' view of mathematics as an interconnected web of concepts can be nurtured by making explicit links between mathematical contexts and one way of doing this is to devise tasks in which students are aware of using existing skills in new contexts.

It is customary in some classrooms to explore shapes by talking about types and symmetries with a view to creating classroom displays. Below we offer a series of situations that relate superficially to naming shapes and simple symmetries, yet also offer the opportunity to work in progressively more complex ways, such as relating properties of shapes to geometrical facts which can be stated, and perhaps proved, using increasingly precise mathematical language.

In the following set of ideas a range of skills are encountered, practised and consolidated. The starting points are shapes made by joining various triangles together: the $30°$, $60°$, $90°$ triangle, the $45°$, $45°$, $90°$ triangle, the $72°$, $72°$, $36°$ triangle and the $108°$, $36°$, $36°$ triangle (the last two are sometimes called the 'pentagon' triangles).

Some of the linked concepts that can be used are: algebraic coding; calculating angle and angle sum; area; pre-Pythagoras work. Furthermore, if the activity generates several results, students can try to prove the completeness of the set.

The 30°, 60°, 90° triangle

The 30°, 60°, 90° triangle can be made using simple paper folding as follows.

First fold a piece of A4 paper in half vertically (fold line EF); unfold. Then fold corner D onto line EF from corner A. This point will be labelled I. The fold line is AGH.
Fold again, so AH lies along AB, to make fold line AIJ

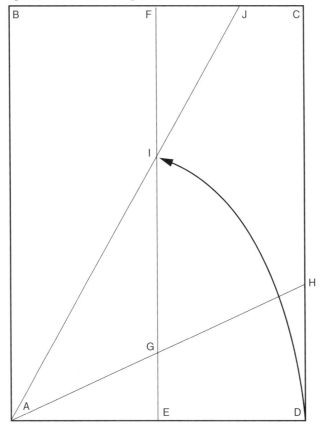

Fig. 8.

We recognize that some people find paper folding very difficult. This difficulty is unrelated to mathematical attainment. It may be sensible to ask students to work in pairs, choosing who folds the paper, and for the teacher to give a mirror image demonstration while giving instructions.

The whole class could be asked what angle DAG is. Intuitively, because the right-angle corner at A has been tri-sected, this is 30°. Students can be asked to check this and to find out why. Some students could prove this fact linking this work to trigonometry. Others might explore whether it will be true for other sizes of paper.

The next task could be to find every angle; there are 22 angles on the sheet so this can offer plenty of practice at working them out. There are also opportunities for students to see the occurrence of 'opposite angles are equal', 'alternate angles are equal', 'angle sum of a triangle is 180°', and so on. The challenge is to see which angles can be found without measuring. Students can be given a writing framework to complete, such as: 'Angle DAG is 30°, so angle ... must be ... degrees because ...'

An extension to this task, which provides opportunities for further practice and consolidation of angles and angle facts, is to fold corner **D** in half and create a 45° angle. By doing this, further angles are added to the sheet:

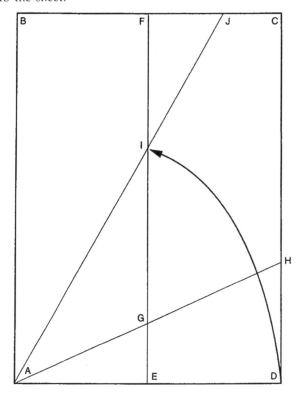

Fig. 9.

Returning to the earlier diagram, a further challenge is to ask students to completely tessellate the piece of paper with 30°, 60°, 90° triangles by further folding, thus replicating triangles DAH, EAI or EAG. An open question about the different shapes students can see on the paper can provide a starting point for a number of explorations about shapes, enlargements and other transformations.

Flipping triangles

This next idea is based upon working with a single 30°, 60°, 90° triangle cardboard template.

By labelling the sides L (longest), M (middle length) and S (shortest), students can explore shapes made by 'flipping' a copy of the triangle over different sides. In the example below, an obtuse-angled isosceles triangle has been formed as a result of flipping a copy over side S. Its perimeter can be written algebraically in terms of L, M, and S. Students can be reminded that perimeter is the distance round the edges by imagining an ant walking along the lines.

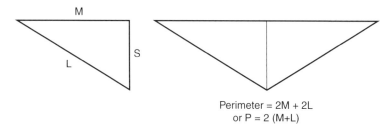

Perimeter = 2M + 2L
or P = 2 (M+L)

Fig. 10.

The ant will travel M + M + L + L. It is an obvious step to use the shorthand version 2M + 2L or 'two lots of M and L = 2 (M + L)'. Algebra is thus introduced naturally as a way to express perimeter.

When all possible shapes have been found using one flip, and they have been named and their perimeters have been expressed, further shapes can be made using two flips. This diagram shows a two-flip triangle, about side **S** and side **L** and its perimeter is 3M + S + L.

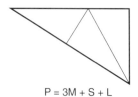

P = 3M + S + L

Fig. 11.

Using this as a starting point, a range of problems can be tackled and different skills can be practised. Some questions and associated content are:

Questions	Mathematical content
What other one and two-flip shapes are there?	Justifying or proving completeness
What are they called?	Properties and names of shapes
What angles does each shape have?	Angle facts
What angle sum does each shape have?	Angle facts
What are the perimeters of each shape, in terms of L, M and S?	Algebraic coding

In this approach, all students can work on all features of simple shapes. Complexity arises naturally as more flips are introduced.

Rotating triangles

Instead of flipping around a side, what shapes can be made if rotations are carried out about the mid-points of sides of the triangle? In the diagram below, the parallelogram has been created by rotating the triangle 180° about the centre of the side marked **S**.

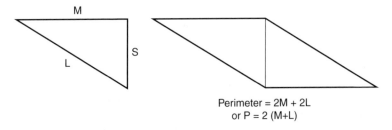

Perimeter = 2M + 2L
or P = 2 (M+L)

Fig. 12.

Similar questions as before can now be asked, for example: how many shapes can be made with one, two, three successive rotations about different midpoints? What happens if the rotations take place around the same midpoint?

One of us overheard a student remark, 'you always have to find "how many?"' In the above examples we have asked 'how many', but we have also asked more challenging questions, and questions which focus on curriculum content. However, the student's comment is a reminder that it is possible to carry out a very limited activity within what the teacher believes to be a rich mathematical environment. The teacher's role is to intervene to ensure that mathematical thinking is always high on the agenda, and to provide other adults with ways to do this by preparing appropriate prompts and challenges in advance. One way to shift the emphasis from generating complete sets to focusing on properties is to ask students to find examples which have particular features. In the case of flipping triangles we might ask, 'can you make a triangle which is three times as large as the original by successive flips?' In the case of rotating triangles we might ask, 'what sort of triangle is required so that a symmetrical hexagon be made by successive rotations?' These questions encourage students to reorganize their knowledge so that they have to conjecture and then test their ideas.

The 45°, 45°, 90° triangle

Below the shapes A, B and C are all made by joining two right-angled isosceles triangles, by edges of equal length.

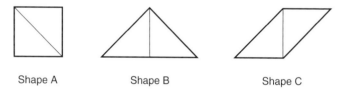

Shape A   Shape B   Shape C

Fig. 13.

The following questions may be considered:

(a) What are the symmetries of the shapes?
(b) What is the angle sum of each shape?
(c) What kind of movements are required to change: shape A to shape B? shape B to shape C? shape A to shape C?
(d) How many shapes can be made by joining three or four such triangles together?
(e) Is there a systematic method for finding all these shapes?

Pythagoras on a 45°, 45°, 90° triangle grid

The grid below can used to explore squares on the sides of right-angled isosceles triangles of various sizes in order to demonstrate special cases of Pythagoras' theorem.

- using properties such as length, area, peri'
  to introduce, through need, algebraic sy'
- using simple examples of concepts wh'
  that there is something familiar to rec
- transforming 'how many' questions ı.
  questions.

REFERENCES

The books 'Geometric Images' (referred to in Chapter 9) and 'Starting Points' (referred to in Chapter 6) were both used in the development of ideas in this chapter.
De Cordova, C., (1983) *The Tessellations File*. Tarquin: Diss

1

pproximations

In several textbooks and schemes of work, 'approximation' appears as a discrete topic. But few students carry what they learn in special lessons on approximation (or any other idea learnt in isolation) into other areas of mathematics. Some even end up with the idea that they are only supposed to think about approximation when specifically asked to do so.

Students have experience of approximation outside mathematics classrooms. Many will have used phrases such as: 'about right', 'give or take a bit', 'roughly' and so on. In lessons, therefore, the focus needs to be on *mathematical* meanings of approximation, and what role approximation plays in mathematics. Approximation is an aspect of all measuring and calculating. It is the flipside of accuracy, and could be considered whenever calculations and measuring are being done. The aim is not, however, to *transfer* knowledge from abstract into concrete situations, but to develop *habits* of approximating which can be brought into play in any context. Nevertheless, it is worth having lessons in which approximation is the explicit focus, so the teacher can be sure that students have had a common experience in this fundamental area and can refer back to the lesson later.

The phrase 'common experience' does not imply 'common understanding'. Each student's view of the lesson will be different; the teacher cannot assume that all students will have learnt the same things. They will all have taken part in the same tasks, and the same whole class discussions, and been exposed to the same language and boardwork, but will come away with varying understandings and memories of the lesson.

A common feature of modern language lessons, which can be usefully adopted by mathematics teachers, is the use of many similar questions, directed at named students, inviting them to respond out loud and hence practise using key words and phrases. This ensures that many students take part directly in the mathematics. Since approximation is a feature of much arithmetic, and of ways to verify reasonableness of answers, it is well worth employing the technique of targeted questioning to ensure that all students, over time, experience it. A useful strategy is to ask everyone to write answers to some questions, such as: 'Approximately how high is the door?'; 'How long is the room?'; 'How many students are in the school?'. Once students have committed themselves to an estimate, several can read them out, without comment from the teacher, but with discussion among students. One aspect which may arise is that estimations are given to different degrees of accuracy, thus giving opportunity to revise work on rounding numbers and to decide what accuracy is appropriate in the context.

We give examples of approximation tasks, but we do not give suggestions for sequences of lessons in this case. We see the occasional lesson, and subsequent incorporation into all aspects of mathematical work, as a more fitting way to treat this feature of mathematics. For example, the work about trigonometry described in Chapter 9 provides a useful context for rounding to two or more decimal places.

ASPECTS TO CONSIDER WHEN TEACHING ESTIMATION

A first consideration is the difference between guessing and estimating. Although these ideas are not clearly distinguishable, it is generally the case that one should be able to give mathematical reasons for estimating, whereas guesses can be somewhat more vague. Estimating leads to an approximation along with some information about its closeness to an accurate value. For instance, consider the following instruction:

Estimate 18×52

An answer of 1000, derived from 20×50, would be an approximation, but is not the only acceptable answer. However, students can work out that it is a closer approximation than 750, obtained from $15 \times 100/2 = 15 \times 50$, or 1100, obtained from $10 \times 55 \times 2$.

A second consideration is that it is a big step for students to understand that there are situations in which answers do not have to be accurate, and there can be many equally acceptable answers. This may involve a major shift in their arithmetical thinking in that they now have to offer possibilities, rather than operate with a prescribed method, to find an answer. A style of questioning in which the teacher is always looking for a particular answer in order to move to the next planned question can often result in only the most confident students volunteering to answer. Many classrooms operate in a way which discourages students from taking risks with answers they are not sure about, so a shift of classroom behaviour is useful. Public questioning, targeted at several students, encourages, values and celebrates this shift. For instance, the teacher might ask:

Alan, can you give me a rough answer to 35 multiplied by 41?
Bonnie, what would your rough answer be?
Callum, give me your estimate for 35 times 41?
Del, approximately, what would 35 lots of 41 be?

Here the teacher is encouraging an approximation to a decontextualized multiplication, perhaps to be done by rounding 41 to 40 and then dealing with 'three tens and half a ten' of 40.

Note that, in this suggestion, the questions are about pure calculation rather than being contextualized for different students. A contextualized version might lead to a very different approach. For example, the question:

About how many people can be carried in 35 buses which each hold up to 41 passengers?

might trigger an additive approach: two buses hold about 80, four buses hold about 160 and so on. Contextualizing the question may, therefore, steer some pupils towards using different methods. The question:

How far would a rabbit move in 41 jumps if each jump is 35 centimetres?

might encourage an experimental approach, or recourse to a scaled number line from 0 to 10 000, if one is available. It is, in our opinion, a good idea to have a variety of number lines around mathematics classrooms. All primary schools in the UK now use them as part of the National Numeracy Strategy.

As a mathematical topic, approximation certainly includes the development of estimates for calculations as described above, but there are other aspects too which need to be recognized and worked on explicitly. For instance, approximation is also a feature of the following mathematical activities, for which examples are given.

Conversion. At the time of writing there are roughly six shekels to one pound sterling, so conversion between currencies can be achieved by the approximate, yet adequate, methods of multiplying or dividing by six and making the necessary place value adjustments.

Measurement. How exact is it possible to be when measuring the playground, or when measuring a geometric figure, or when weighing flour?

Reasonableness of accuracy. How many decimal places is it reasonable to work with when using ratio of sides to calculate an angle?

Iterative solution of equations. What might be lost or gained by rounding to four significant figures at each stage of an iteration when using a spreadsheet? Would inaccuracies increase unacceptably as the iteration proceeds?

Conjecturing. Give 'ball-park' figures in mathematical situations, such as guessing the perimeter of the fifth shape in a sequence, knowing the perimeters of the fourth and sixth shapes.

For one word to relate to so many different activities is a potential source of confusion as well as a rich source of possibilities in the classroom. Sometimes approximation is about seeing, sometimes about producing answers, and sometimes about use. These different ideas can be discussed with students to help them make decisions about the place of approximation in their mathematics.

EXAMPLES OF APPROXIMATION BY SEEING

Geometrically

In the context of a geometrical diagram: 'It looks as if this is a right angle'.

We may not be sure about geometric properties by looking or measuring, but the conjecture that an angle *might* be is 90° may lead us to check by other means, by appeal to geometric facts or reasoning. Of course, just because a geometric diagram *looks* as if it contains right angles, or equal lines, does not mean that it is intended to represent these features. The use of 'it looks as if' might mislead students to assume some geometric properties or symmetries which are not intended. This kind of misreading is common so can be used in class to highlight the dangers of assumption. Examination candidates frequently make specific assumptions from diagrams which are intended to be general, rather than to represent actual lengths and angles.

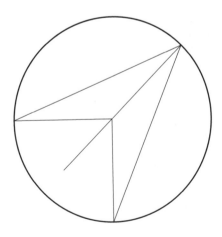

Fig. 16.

Statements about comparable lengths and angles need to be verified, perhaps by using geometry software or construction. This can lead to useful discussion and further activities.

Graphically

In the context of seeing where a graph cuts the x-axis. 'It looks as if it is near 3.5'.

This observation gives a useful starting point for iteration, a value of x which can be substituted into the equation of the graph to see if it really does give $y = 0$, and to suggest how to reach a better degree of accuracy if not.

Numerically

In the context of using a number line to estimate, visually, something like 0.6 × 3.5. 'It looks as if it will be somewhere around 2'.

This approach, using three and a half segments of length 0.6 on a number line to visualize multiplication, can, over time, help students to establish for themselves rules for decimal multiplication and division. The idea is that the naive concept of multiplication as repeated addition can be used. One can visualize 0.6 as a little over half and then imagine marking off three-and-a-half lots of 0.6 along the number line.

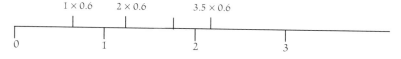

We can imagine another way to approximate in this case by using the commutativity of multiplication.

Measuring

In the context of measuring. 'It looks as if it is about 5 metres high'.

Students may have a mental image of a metre, or may have to hand another object which they know to be n metres in length. If the measuring device is vertical and the object to be measured is horizontal, such as when using one's own height to estimate the width of a room, visual estimation can be misleading and this would be worth exploring further.

We do not see this kind of approximation as problematic for *any* student, so long as it is approached in a spirit of fun. For instance, it is likely that a track athlete might be a lot better at seeing 100 metres than a student who never does athletics. There is no need to confine 'seeing' just to visual senses; the same kinds of questions can be posed and worked on by touch, or in the imagination. For example:

Imagine a healthy apple tree ten feet high and eight feet across at its widest. How many apples might it carry?

APPROXIMATIONS CONTRIBUTING TO FINDING ANSWERS

All calculations can be preceded by estimating the expected size of the answer so that the subsequent calculation, whether done mentally, by written algorithm or with technological help, can be verified from number sense or common sense. The reverse is also useful: where common sense can be misleading a prior estimate can show the mismatch and help the teacher notice what needs to be worked on further. For instance, if a learner assumes that multiplication always increases values, and therefore wrongly estimates the answer to multiplications by numbers less than 1, the 'estimate-check' approach can lead the student to the realization that her strongly persistent image of increase has to be changed.

Approximations are frequently used outside classrooms when converting from one kind of unit to another. A traditional approach to conversion would involve ratio, but in practice people use a range of 'rules of thumb'. An approach that could include all students would be to ask them to bring to school examples of: the ways they convert foreign currency if they holiday abroad; ways in which anyone who cooks in their family converts recipe quantities; equivalent measures displayed on food packaging, petrol pumps, speedometers, school rulers; 'rules of thumb' used by people involved in trades or sports activities. These could be used to generate questions such as

If one dollar is worth 60p, how much are two dollars worth?

Conversion tables can be created and displayed on the wall. For example, one could have tables for grams to pounds, centimetres to inches, litres to gallons and vice versa. Useful multiples can include those which can be combined to provide ways to calculate other values. For instance it is useful to have multiples such as: two times, ten times, 100 times, half, a tenth and so on displayed on posters. These tables can be augmented and used in future lessons. They can also provide the raw material for later work on ratios or for interpretation of graphs by creating conversion graphs.

USING APPROXIMATIONS IN MATHEMATICAL LEARNING

Example (i)

In the context of solving an equation, some of the coefficients and constants can be rounded in order to make it easy to solve for approximate answers, which can be used as starting points for iteration. This method does not always work, because some equations are badly behaved and small changes in coefficients can create large variations in iterative sequences. For example, the iterative approach to solving the equation $x = 3.5x (1 - x)$ is significantly different from that of solving $x = 3.54x (1 - x)$. Hence working with such methods can lead to some students beginning to understand chaotic situations while others are working on developing guess-and-check methods. The teacher might provide a class with a variety of equations to solve, linear and quadratic, and a variety of possible methods of generating a first approximation. For instance, students could plot graphs and see where equality occurs, or do a rough calculation, or generate values of a function on a spreadsheet and see which input values give a result close to equality, and so on.

Students might work on a common core of questions, and then be given a range of follow-up tasks, depending on their progress.

Example (ii)

Using an approximation as a starting point, a class might be given a number and asked to suggest what numbers could be represented by it, with the appropriate approximation rule. For example, given 10, students might say, '*it can represent 7, but not 4, to the nearest ten*', or '*9.6 to the nearest whole number*' or '*8, but not 7, to the nearest multiple of five*' and so on. Such an activity can be a useful whole class discussion; a variety of different degrees of comprehension can be incorporated into it.

Example (iii)

Whenever we measure anything, the answer is necessarily approximate, so all measuring activities can be accompanied by discussion about sensible degrees of accuracy.

Using measurements as the data for further calculations can throw up some interesting issues. For example, using the ratio of measured sides to calculate an angle can be accompanied by discussion about the sensibleness of giving an answer to several decimal places as found on a calculator. The same kind of discussion could accompany the results of a division, or square-root of a measured value. The technique of asking what would happen if the measured value is 0.5 units too small, or too big, can be used to show students how to use approximations sensibly.

A whole class approach might be to ask students to work out, on their calculators, a range of values such as:

inv sin (3.55/6.25), inv sin (3.55/6.26), inv sin (3.55/6.27), inv sin (3.54/ 6.25) . . .

This exercise will generate a range of answers from which students, as a class, can pick out the common features as the most sensible approximation. It also gives practice in how to explore systematically a situation with two variables. Not all students will fully grasp the complexity of this task, but all might at least appreciate a need for caution when using measurements, a sense of finding commonalities in a range of numbers, and practice in an aspect of trigonometry.

A simpler situation, involving multiplication, is to consider a calculation such as 3.5×11.5. Does 3×12 or 4×11 give the closest answer? This problem can be developed to include algebraic problems.

Consider $(a + 0.5)$ degrees $\times (b + 0.5)$, where $a < b$.

Think about potential approximations: $(a + 1) \times b$ and $a \times (b + 1)$: which gives the best approximation? which gives the largest answer?

Example (iv)

Another situation in which measuring errors can be discussed is when measuring a cereal packet to calculate its volume. This calculation can precede discussion about the relationship between the actual contents and the size of the box. However, the accuracy of the measurements is constrained by the marks on the ruler and it might be interesting to work out the maximum volume error resulting from a slight reading error. Suppose the reading error is taken to be ± 0.5 cm, then it might be useful to draw attention to the resultant volume error, both in absolute and relative terms.

Students will be intrigued that error bounds are added both when lengths are added or subtracted. Calculating the maximum possible errors in such calculations will, for most students, contradict their intuitive notions. For example, if a length of 5 cm $\pm$ 0.5 cm is cut from a length of 12 cm $\pm$ 0.5 cm the maximum possible error is 1.0 cm, assuming the smallest possible length of one and the largest possible length of the other.

Example (v)

A final example, and one which we feel should be incorporated into all calculations, is to encourage students to suggest approximate answers before they carry out a calculation. Often this will entail rounding the given numbers and doing a rough calculation; sometimes it entails imagining the context of the question and what they might do in reality. For instance, questions about shopping appear frequently in national tests but not all students imagine themselves shopping as an aid to choosing how to calculate answers. In non-school situations, people seldom multiply and divide. More frequently they use a mixture of methods and a sense of getting close to an answer. In our experience, there is frequent confusion between multiplication and division when students are given written, contextualized questions. Sometimes students have been given rules to follow such as, 'if it says "how much", you times the numbers; if it says "how many", you share the numbers'. Much research has been done on the errors and confusions that can result in this kind of question. Our approach would be to encourage the imagination, even by role play, and use the students' outside experience not to give an accurate method but to help them choose which operation to perform. The use of the calculator here allows the accurate answer to be produced, the approximation allows it to be checked. We maintain that having many experiences of having to choose operations in differently structured questions enables students to make better choices in future without the need to approximate first.

STRATEGIES USED IN THIS CHAPTER

- setting practice in a mathematical context, not as an isolated skill;
- targeting questions to individuals;
- helping students develop mathematical habits;
- asking the same question in a variety of forms;
- recognizing that different contexts can prompt different approaches;
- using students' special knowledge;
- getting students to use imagination to think themselves into a situation;
- estimating used to verify calculation, and vice versa;
- practising choosing operations and methods;
- using examples brought from home;
- having wall-displays of work-in-progress;
- using different examples of the same concept, each having a different pedagogic intention;
- varying the difficulty of examples, have some for practice and some to challenge;
- asking questions which can be answered at a variety of levels;
- getting the whole class to generate a data set for discussion;

- giving tasks which model how to work with mathematical problem-solving;
- sometimes using algebra as incidental to the main explanation.

REFERENCES

Corte, E. D. and Verschaffel, L. (1991) 'Some factors influencing the solution of addition and subtraction problems'. This is a chapter in the book by Durkin and Shire which we used in Chapter 4. It gives useful insights into how students think about which operation to use.

Area

When approaching area at any stage of secondary education it is worthwhile to acknowledge that students will have prior knowledge. Typically, they will have had colouring, counting and cutting experiences relating to area. They may have attempted to apply formulae such as 'base times height'. Often such formulae will be misapplied, leading to an apparently random multiplying of lengths for any planar shape with straight sides. Consequently students will arrive in secondary school with a range of perceptions about the concept. In our view, what is required at secondary level is experience in exploring areas of shapes in a variety of ways, allowing four central issues to be addressed: what area means; how it is conserved; the fact that area and perimeter are not related; and understanding how to calculate area. Revisiting and practising calculations for area can take place within problem-solving contexts so that the teacher can give specific help as and when it is needed. We give a typical web of ideas in Figure 17.

GRAZING PROBLEMS

In many textbooks it is common for area and perimeter to be treated together. This can be a source of confusion for students who have a clear image of the concept of length, with the word 'measure' indicating a linear scale. Often the concept of area is not so clear, and the question 'How can we measure the area?' is confusing.

There are some traditional grazing problems that allow all these aspects to be included. Some of these are about sheep grazing in fields constrained by sheep pens of a particular perimeter:

A farmer has fencing 36 metres long. It can be arranged in any shape to make a grazing pen for a few sheep. What is the maximum area which can be grazed?

There is always the possibility that contexts are unhelpful. Farmers do not really do the calculations intended by this question; also some fencing acts as if continuous and some as discrete lengths. A teacher may prefer to work within the context of mathematics and ask:

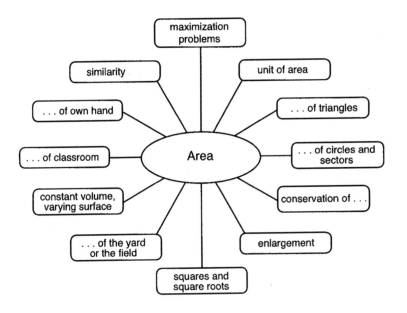

Fig. 17.

How many different shapes can be made with a perimeter of 36 cm? What are their areas?

Various ways to arrange the fencing to make a rectangular pen can be explored using a spreadsheet. This question can be extended by including a stream in the pasture, or an obstacle such as the corner of a barn, which makes the 'best' rectangular solution (a 6 metre by 6 metre square) impossible. Students will have to practise their use of rectangular area formula, and with the added constraints may have to calculate areas compounded of several rectangles. They will have to decide how to split a compound shape into simpler parts, and different choices can be compared and evaluated. Of course, there is no requirement to make the pen rectangular, and attempts to find areas of other polygons may lead to a need for scale drawings or the use of trigonometric ratios to find heights of triangles which form part of the polygons.

Suppose the area is kept constant and different rectangles are drawn. It will be found that many different perimeters are possible, including a minimum value. If other shapes are explored it might be found that a circle gives the minimum perimeter for a given area.

One of our reasons for offering the sheep-grazing problems is that they give opportunities to work explicitly on the conceptual confusions of students. Exploring the lack of clear relationships between area and perimeter is of intellectual interest to some students, but may not help those who are unsure what area means. As in all mathematics, the teacher needs to intervene to help students think about, and articulate, their understanding of what area is and what the constituent units of area are, i.e. how it is 'measured'.

Another set of grazing problems is couched in terms of a goat tethered to some part of a field:

A goat is to be tethered in a square field of edge 10 metres. There is a diagonal path running between opposite corners of the field. The goat is only allowed to eat the grass on one side of the path. Where should the goat be tethered so that it can reach the maximum amount of grass? What is the maximum area the goat can graze?

Here the idea is to calculate the area the goat can graze subject to the length of the tether and some other constraints. In fact, such problems also allow students to get a sense of loci too, particularly if the goat is on a running, rather than fixed, tether.

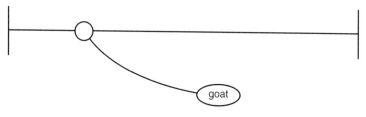

Fig. 18.

The problem can be posed in a practical way, using models, string and drawing pins to provide the tether. Students can offer suggestions about where the tether might be fixed and estimates of greater or lesser areas can be made. Such a shared approach helps all students to get started on the problem, because they have heard the ideas of others and can try them out, or attempt to do better.

Mathematical issues arising from goat-tethering problems

Several mathematical issues may arise, according to the approach a student might take. For example, students will need to decide how to draw appropriate diagrams; this will include the appreciation that compasses will have to be used to provide the drawn model of the extent of the goat's grazing.

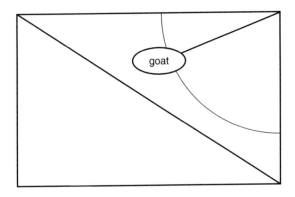

Fig. 19.

Working on squared paper allows students to estimate the grazed area for each position they try; is it necessary to calculate the area exactly for each position, or will an estimate do? The teacher may decide that some students should do the calculations because it is good practice, but this insistence might be demotivating for them. If a student soon finds a maximum, and can justify it, how can practice through repetitive examples be provided? The teacher will have to decide if this student really needs to practise. If so, then further questions can be posed such as: Where can the goat be tethered so that the area it grazes is one quarter of the whole field? Where can the goat be placed on a running tether so that it grazes the maximum possible area without crossing a path or stream?

Calculation of areas of sectors can be done by finding fractions of circles. Many students may need at this stage to be told the way to calculate areas of circles. We are in favour of telling students such facts if by doing so the student can work on the wider problem without interrupting the flow of the lesson.

For some positions of the tether the resultant area will consist of a sector (or some sectors) of a circle and some residual triangles. The teacher can give a method for finding areas of sectors and triangles where the apex is known. Alternatively the altitudes of triangles can be found by measuring on a scale drawing, or by a trigonometric calculation if appropriate angles are known. Again, it is up to the teacher to decide whether to tell a student how to do these calculations if they have chosen this approach, or to guide them towards a scale drawing and measuring approach if it seems more appropriate and accessible.

More adaptations of these problems include the goat being tethered to the corner of a square shed, a rectangular shed, or even a circular shed. This version provides challenges for the very strongest students. A further challenge would be to tether the goat to the fence of a circular field and arrange for it to graze half the field. This last challenge presents significant modelling problems, can be a good introduction to the need for numerical methods, and requires some knowledge of circle theorems. As far as we know the problem cannot be solved algebraically.

EXPLORING AREA IN INCLUSIVE CLASSROOMS

This kind of classroom organization, in which all students are working on the same problem, from the same starting point, but pursuing different questions within it, is fundamental to the management of inclusive classrooms. It is perfectly possible for a teacher to vary the questions and constraints to challenge all students, and to arrange for practice of a variety of area calculations. However, the responsibility for this can also be handed over to the students. For example, they can be asked to 'think up a field-and-fence or tether arrangement which forces the class to calculate lots of areas of triangles'; 'think of a situation' which requires the trapezium formula' ... and so on.

In nearly all the cases described above, some students could still count squares if using the formula does not seem appropriate, but in our experience, and particularly with the use of information technology, such as spreadsheets, to evaluate formulae, all students can handle some of the calculations. The presence of some students using formulae provides a model for others of the efficiency and speed of their use compared to a counting approach.

In earlier parts of this book we mention how important it is for students to understand the mathematics they are doing, and it may seem that some of what we have said here about telling them how to calculate areas goes against that. However, inclusion can take a variety of forms, and sometimes the confidence that can be attained by getting right answers, particularly in a shared context, can be empowering enough to give students a feeling of achievement that carries over into harder aspects of their work. Understanding need not precede use; in fact, there is a kind of understanding that could be described as 'understanding when and how to use ...' rather than understanding from first principles or through derivation. One reaches a kind of understanding of a tool by using it. There are several instances in this book where we show that telling students how to calculate something they need might be a more motivating pedagogic decision than avoiding the calculation, or expecting them to use ad hoc methods.

We do not consider it to be the case that the above collection of tasks is the only work done on area. The experience of several approaches enriches understanding in ways that cannot necessarily be predicted by the teacher. The above tasks provide opportunities for students to think about areas, to practise using a variety of area formulae, to relate them to perimeter, to think about how they might be formed, to realize that areas can be found by adding (or subtracting) areas of their constituent shapes, to find fractions of areas, to construct fractions as appropriate, to meet and use trigonometry to find unknown lengths, to measure lengths and angles, to estimate areas using square grids, to make up their own related questions aimed at using given formulae, to justify when they claim to have reached a maximum, possibly using spreadsheets or graphs to help them find or communicate their findings.

The warning that context might mislead students is important to remember throughout the ideas above. The situations are unrealistic; it is one of the features of mathematics that we sometimes work with unrealistic situations. There should be no pretence that this is how real farmers make real decisions about grazing. Students need to enter into the fiction and use the tether as a device to think about radius, and the constraints as devices for them to play with mathematical constraints.

STRATEGIES USED IN THIS CHAPTER

- creating mathematical situations in which repeated calculations, hence practice, *have* to take place;
- posing a problem in ways which encourage engagement of all students;
- sharing ideas about how to get started;
- giving tasks which have several ways forward;
- giving tasks which give space for students to construct meaning, such as through estimating before calculating, or through combining smaller areas to find larger areas;
- students choosing different approaches;
- teacher choosing whether to tell useful formulae or not;
- pointing out explicit links within mathematics;
- asking for justification;
- extending situations by developing more constraints;
- limiting the scope of an exploration to ensure certain areas of mathematics are worked on;
- creating challenges for all;
- asking the whole class to generate examples of practice problems;
- incorporating information technology into mathematical work.

REFERENCES

Dudeney, H. E. (1917) *Amusements in Mathematics.* London: Nelson. This author's collections of activities are well worth looking for in secondhand shops.

Mason, J. with Burton, L. and Stacey, K. (1982) *Thinking Mathematically.* London: Addison-Wesley.

—13

Geometrical proof

Geometrical proof forms a major part of the secondary geometry curriculum in many countries. In the UK, however, it has largely been excluded from the National Curriculum until the time of writing (2000). In its place has been an approach to geometry which concentrates on properties of shape and space, measures, transformations, and conjectures based on similarity, symmetry and congruence. 'Shape and space', as it is described in the UK national curriculum, is not necessarily treated in a rigorous way. Students may be left with the idea that measuring confirms a property, or that a description of properties is enough to define a shape, or that arguments based on symmetries (translation, rotation and reflection) in a particular case can constitute a proof. The introduction of dynamic geometry software, while offering many opportunities for development of rigorous argument, might leave an impression that demonstration by using a movable diagram is all that is required for proof.

In this section we assume that geometrical proof, as part of the cultural history of mathematics, has a place in a school curriculum. We describe approaches which take into account the difficulties learners traditionally have with understanding the need for proof, and in producing their own proofs. We also talk about the power and appeal of transformational arguments and the use of dynamic geometry.

The network overleaf links together so many features of a school mathematics curriculum that it makes no sense to deal with proof as a separate topic. Proof is an overarching mathematical activity, like calculation or measuring, and hence we include it as part of *all* work on shape and space. The network gives clues about how proof might be introduced if we begin to question how links can be made between various items. For example, in any geometrical situation we could ask:

What conjectures might be made? What might be seen? What can be deduced from what is already known?

Obviously this sequence of questions has to apply to some shapes, so we could apply it several times during the secondary school curriculum: with quadrilaterals and triangles, polygons, regular and irregular shapes, circles and more complex figures such as diagrams of angles in circles.

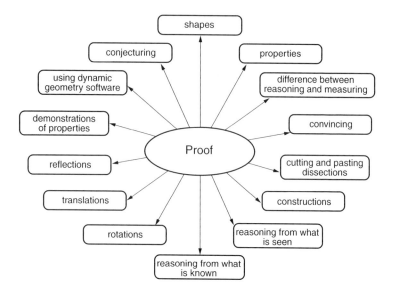

Fig. 20.

Applying these questions to those quadrilaterals with special names leads us to list the properties which we might like to explore in class. We aim to create precise and full descriptions of quadrilaterals so we can discriminate between them. We could look at angles, sides, diagonals, parallelism, equalities, inequalities and relationships between features.

STARTING WITH INFORMAL DISCUSSIONS

Since we want to start from what is most familiar to pupils, we start with a whole class session in which students give information about the properties of a square. To introduce the need for convincing argument at this stage we ask, for each property given, how many ways students can use to convince each other. For example, here is a typical snippet of interaction from a lesson about showing that all sides of a square are equal:

Pupil 1:   *All the sides are equal.*
Teacher: *Can anyone convince me?*
Pupil 2:   *Measure them.*
Teacher: *Will that work for all squares? Another way?*
Pupil 3:   *Use a stick the same length and put it against each side.*
Teacher: *Will that work for all squares? Another way?*

Pupil 4: *Draw it on squared paper.*
Teacher: *Will that work for all squares? Another way?...*
Can you suggest a way using compasses?...
Can you suggest a way using paper-folding?

This example shows how the teacher can introduce techniques for geometrical working through gentle prompts, encouraging students to think of less familiar techniques for themselves. In this snippet there is the suggestion that students ought to look for a range of different examples and counter-examples. If students are always asked to look for examples and counter-examples they may begin to do this autonomously and this will help them to become precise in their descriptions. Drawing a square on squared paper will not be helpful if the side is not an integer, or is too large for the paper, or does not need to have edges parallel to the edge of the paper. On the other hand, drawing a tilted square on squared paper can introduce students to the relationship between the sides of a right-angled triangle.[1]

The teacher is also aware that students need to know that the function of compasses is to give equal lengths, and takes the opportunity to remind them about this. The hint about 'folding' relates to approaches to geometry in which shapes are overlaid onto each other to show equality of lengths or angles (see diagrams below). This approach can be linked to dissection proofs and transformational arguments. In this case, cutting a square into two right-angled isosceles congruent triangles can open the way to several arguments about equality, such as equality of diagonals, equality of areas. Cutting can also lead to discussion about what one has to do to one triangle to overlay it onto the other; for the square a reflection (fold) is enough, but for a rectangle a rotation has to be done.

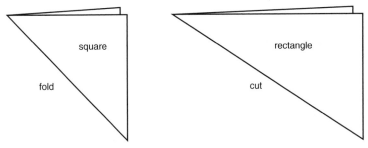

Fig. 21.

From the initial discussion about squares, students can work on a variety of tasks. The interchange between the teacher and the whole class can 'set the scene' for good ways to work with geometry and generate ways in which students can convince each other about properties. Students could try to construct a square using one or two of the properties given, either using compass and ruler or using software. This experience can lead to discussion about how many, and which, properties are enough to describe a square. We have found all students of secondary age able to do this, to a greater or lesser extent, because the square is such a familiar object. Some students may need help with the physical aspects of drawing; they could work in pairs so only one has to draw while the other hypothesizes. Thus students are introduced to ideas of necessity and sufficiency in geometric argument, as well as learning more about ways to construct shapes. Similar ways of working can be applied to other quadrilaterals and triangles, while students build up for themselves a record of shapes and their properties, frequently being expected to demonstrate and convince each other of what they have found.

So far the plans suggested here have not included any formal proving, but have included many of the visual and physical aspects of working geometrically which were excluded by traditional, formal approaches.

SHIFTING TO FORMAL REASONING

A serious problem with the shift required to use classical geometrical reasoning is that it depends on acceptance of certain axioms, coupled with a pretence that nothing else is known about the shapes being considered. In other words, one might have to pretend that one does not know the diagonals of a square are equal, although it is perfectly obvious they are by sight, and easy to argue that they are by symmetry. One might be tempted to argue by contradiction, saying, 'if they were not equal, one diagonal would push its vertices out further than the other, so ...' Instead, one has to use the axioms together with 'facts' which have already been proved, and suspend any intuitive or visual knowledge. One way we have used to do this has been to collect initial assumptions and proved facts in a class list and displayed them on the classroom wall. These might be described as 'Proof Tools'.

Newly proved facts can be added to the list, and students can be asked to convince each other of 'new' properties by using only the facts on the class list. This constrains the student to what is accepted as known, in a classical sense, and gives them the experience of working in this restricted, formal way. Classically, Euclid started with assumptions about points and lines and deduced facts about angles meeting at a point, angles making straight lines, parallel lines

PROOF TOOLS

Parallel lines never meet

Angles on a straight line add up to 180 degrees

Angles meeting at a point add up to 360 degrees

Alternate angels are equal

Corresponding angels are equal

Angles of a triangle add up to 180 degrees

Triangles are congruent if they have some corresponding features:
  a.a.s, s.s.s, s.a.s, r.h.s

Opposite sides of a parallelogram are equal in length

Fig. 22.

(although his axiom for parallel lines was later questioned), and conditions for congruence. A sense that three particular pieces of information are sufficient for complete equality of triangles can be developed through investigation with card shapes.

The following grid of intersecting parallel lines in three directions provides opportunities to move triangle templates around, translating and rotating until all equal angles have been found, described and named.

This grid provides raw material for several conjectures about angles and parallel lines, sums of interior and exterior angles of polygons which are concealed in the grid and so on. Indeed some students may accept these demonstrations as proofs, so it is important that proof by formal reasoning is discussed in class. Students talk about their reasoning and are asked to challenge and improve each others' proofs.

Starting with these tools, several simple proofs can be developed, but most have to start with some sort of construction. During a module on geometry one of us was asked:

Why do we have to construct? How do we know what to construct? Do we just have to learn off by heart what construction to do?

The answer to the first question helps answer the other two. Constructions are done before proof begins so that we can use what we already know to tell us something about a new situation. The objective of the construction is to change an unfamiliar or complex situation into simpler and more familiar parts. For example, suppose we want to prove that the angles of a triangle add up to $180°$ using,

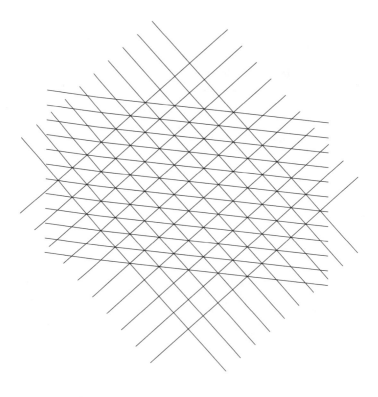

Fig. 23.

as Euclid did, only what we know about parallel lines and angles forming a straight line. In a triangle we do not have any parallel lines, so we must add them somehow. Once we have chosen how to add some parallel lines to the diagram, we can see whether that tells us anything useful about the angles. Students can draw triangles, add parallel lines to their diagrams, see what can be deduced in terms of equal angles and angle sums, and the most useful construction – drawing a line through one vertex parallel to the opposite side – is likely to emerge from the class. Students can then label equal angles and list angle sums until a proof is reached.

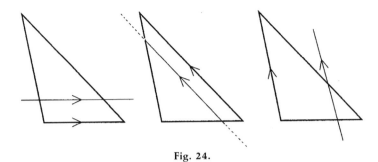

Fig. 24.

This informal approach to formal proof allows all students to be involved, provides frequent opportunity for the constraints of proof to be experienced and avoids the hierarchical notion that proof may only be appropriate for certain 'brighter' students. By making formal proof an activity that is accessible to all we are also making available a cultural tradition which is often seen as elitist and exclusive.

You can probably see for yourself various pathways that might be set up and offered to different students within the general framework we have described.

In much the same way as one expects different responses to a Shakespeare play, it is unrealistic to expect all students to be able to produce formal proofs. However, it is worth striving to make formal proof accessible in the hope that more students might appreciate part, if not all, of the experience of working with it. Puzzle, intrigue and detective work can be used as powerful motivators.

STRATEGIES USED IN THIS CHAPTER

- discussion of what is seen, what is known, what conjectures can be made;
- listing properties of shapes, and relationships between them;
- whole class sharing ways of convincing, and trying them out;
- looking for examples and counter-examples;
- folding/cutting to explore properties of quadrilaterals;
- constructing shapes using known properties;
- repeating the above activities with other shapes;
- demonstrating properties and arguments to each other in pairs or small groups;
- collecting a class 'facts list' of known geometric axioms and properties;
- using a grid made of intersecting parallel lines to explore relationships between angles;

- trying out different constructions to see which is most useful in a proof.

NOTE

1. See Banwell *et al.* (referred to in Chapter 5)

REFERENCES

In June 1996 the journal *Mathematics Teaching* devoted an issue (155) to teaching proof.

14

Fractions and decimals

It is useful to consider different meanings, contexts and notations of fractions. For example, rather than presenting fractions and decimals separately, giving the illusion that they are different, we might pose questions such as:

What is 1¼ of 2.4?

This question once prompted the comment: 'This isn't fair because you have mixed up fractions and decimals' which shows a dependence on form rather than meaning.

Understanding fractions is not straightforward. Teachers frequently shift between different meanings for fractions. They may be seen as numbers on a continuum, such as a number line, or as ordered pairs of integers, or as discrete entities, or as part measures of other quantities, or as operators. Experience tells mathematicians when it is easier to use fractions in one form or when another. For example, when calculating 1¼ of 2.4 it is useful to see the first fraction as representing 'one and a quarter parts of 2.4'; however, if asked the question '2 −1¼ 'it may be more useful to imagine positions on a number line.

Fractions play roles in computations, in the study of rational and irrational numbers, within trigonometry, as indices, as graphs of functions, in mensuration and so on. The teacher's job is to find ways of helping students gain familiarity with fractions in all these contexts and meanings, and as an abstract structure, and be able to transfer their recognition of fractions as a notation and structure between different contexts. Over-reliance on an image of a fraction as a slice of pizza can be an obstacle!

The ideas in this chapter look at one way of getting students to connect concepts of fractions and decimals. Extension from an initial task opens up opportunities to develop ideas of gradients, reciprocals, adding and subtracting fractions.

One possible starting point is to use Cuisenaire rods (or other rods which have values represented by their relative lengths). Cuisenaire rods are of different lengths and colours and are often used to represent numbers, a white rod of length 1 being half the length of the red rod which represents 2, and so on. Here we are interested in their relative lengths in comparison with each other, rather than their absolute lengths.

CUISENAIRE FRACTIONS

Starting with one white and one red rod, the following statements can be written:

$$w = \tfrac{1}{2}r \qquad \text{leading to} \qquad w/r = \tfrac{1}{2};$$

and

$$r = 2w \qquad \text{leading to} \qquad r/w = \tfrac{2}{1}.$$

Students can then explore such statements about fractions using, for example, pairs of six rods from white to turquoise: $\{w, r, g, p, y, t\}$ where red, green, pink, yellow and turquoise are 2, 3, 4, 5 and 6 times as long as white. After students have generated some examples the teacher can guide the discussion towards equivalence and order of fractions. Also vocabulary such as *inverse*, *numerator* and *denominator* can be used explicitly by the teacher and students, and the precise use of 'half' and 'quarter' can be compared to their everyday, informal, uses.

FRACTIONS AS DECIMALS

Some students will already know the decimal equivalents of some of the fractions they have constructed. Finding out the collective knowledge within the classroom of fraction-to-decimal conversions will be useful and one way to proceed is to ask everyone to privately write down all they know about connections between fractions and their decimal equivalents. This information can be pooled without the teacher asking for 'hands-up'. Instead several individuals can be asked to offer what they have written down. Alternatively, after a short period of private, individual writing, students can be asked to share what they have written with one or two other students and then all these ideas can be pooled. This kind of strategy can be applied to a variety of starting lessons to value what students already know. The approach can be adapted for the final five minutes of a lesson by asking a class to write notes about anything they know about the topic of the next lesson. This information can be used to inform the teacher's planning.

Writing fractions as decimal fractions

This task is intended to develop and consolidate students' concepts of fractions as decimal fractions.

The previously-gained information about fractions and their decimal equivalents is transferred onto a 2 cm square dot coordinate grid as below:

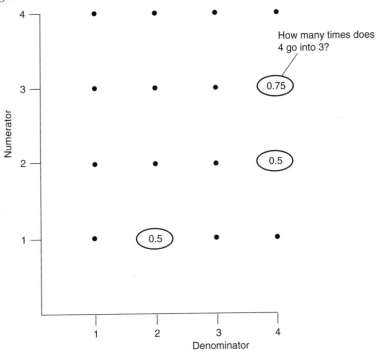

Fig. 25.

One way to do this would be for the teacher to demonstrate how to place the answer to 'how many times does two go into one?' on a grid on the OHP. Students have their own copy of the grid and copy the answer onto it. The teacher does two more points and then students continue on their own. They are asked to do as many as possible before using the calculator, and the teacher reinforces the language structure of the questions in one-to-one interactions. Conveniently, the dots on the grid become decimal points. In order to be consistent, the calculation of a decimal is always structured by the same question format, so that in the case of ½ a horizontal shift of 2 across followed by a vertically upward shift of 1 represents the usual coordinate convention.

Note that the vertical line through the $x = 2$ ordinate will contain the fractions: 0, 0.5, 1.0, 1.5 (going upwards). Students may see the pattern and use it to continue the grid. The pattern can be used as a focus for discussion and some may be able to explain why it occurs. While working on their own the teacher encourages students to see and use patterns and mental methods before resorting to a calculator.

Deciding upon the appropriateness of using a calculator in order to work out some of the more complex decimal equivalents is a typical kind of pedagogic decision. This decision will vary with the context and the teacher's aims. Sometimes pencil-and-paper techniques interrupt the flow of an interesting piece of work; at other times they may provide insight into the task. Whatever decision is made, it will be useful for students to have strategies to be able to calculate the decimal equivalents of a range of fractions.

An interesting result arises when the values on the vertical line through the $x = 3$ ordinate are considered. Students may see that incremental steps of $\frac{1}{3}$ produce: 0.3 recurring, 0.6 recurring and 1 whereas following the numerical pattern would give 0.9 recurring The possibility that 0.9 recurring equals 1 can be discussed, or written as a conjecture on a poster and left for future attention.

Having established the procedure for filling in decimal values, students can complete the rest of the grid.

From this starting point fractions can be ordered according to their size as numbers. Students have to reach some understanding that the size of a decimal number is not related to the number of digits and this can be done through an ordering activity as a whole class. A record of the order can be produced on a number line strip which can be displayed on the classroom wall for later additions and discussion. The order is unrelated to the size of the rods used to form the fractions originally, so there could be discussion in which students try to articulate why this should be. This involves students talking about relative lengths and ratio. Since these aspects of mathematics are hard to express, some students may feel excluded if the whole class approach goes on for too long. It may be better for the teacher to follow up a brief whole class discussion with small group discussions.

Extension tasks

Extending the grid to 12 by 12, for example, enables further explorations to be developed such as:

(i)   exploring recurring decimals: when working with sevenths it is valuable to use pencil-and-paper methods so that students can see that the carrying numbers are remainders, taking all values from 1 to 6, cyclically;

(ii)   equivalence of fractions: straight lines through the origin pass through equivalent fractions;

(iii) finding how gradients of straight lines relate to the coordinates on them.

The 12-by-12 grid can also be used to explore adding or subtracting fractions using the following procedure:

To add $\frac{1}{2}$ and $\frac{2}{5}$ together:

> Find their decimal equivalents on the grid (i.e. 0.5 and 0.4)
> Add these decimal values together to make 0.9
> Find 0.9 on the grid and decode this as a fraction i.e. $\frac{9}{10}$
> Relate $\frac{9}{10}$ to the original two fractions.

This approach is only obvious with simple fractions, but an exploration of why $\frac{1}{2} + \frac{1}{3} = 0.833 \ldots$ would be interesting. Some students might construct a general argument for adding fractions from this experience; for others, this does *not* serve as a way of learning 'how to do it' but gives a sense of what adding fractions is about. Most students will need additional experiences of this topic. Readers may like to use the equivalence classes represented by lines through the origin to devise a method which follows the traditional algorithm.

Complicated recurring decimal fractions are less easy to deal with. However, tasks can legitimately require students to contend with difficulties and try to make sense of complex situations as a result of their exploration. Students' intuitions and conjectures sometimes only work in a narrow range of cases and need to be made more precise, or re-articulated, for other cases. This task is also an example of a situation in which exploration with different tools (calculator, spreadsheet, pencil-and-paper, the grid, their own devised procedures and so on) can give different insights about fractions.

Some students could reflect lines in $y = x$, and see how this relates to reciprocity. In the case illustrated $\frac{1}{2}$ and $\frac{2}{1}$ can be seen to be reciprocals, the y-value taking the place of the x-value and vice versa. Exploring gradients, as tangents of angles, is particularly interesting here.

Students can be encouraged to write about the work they have done and use their diagrams to illustrate this for display. Prepared A4 sheets with square-dot grids based on 2 cm spacing can be useful for students to record the results of their explorations. Alternatively grids with different numbers of dots can be created with the zoom button on the photocopier. Using much larger grids with (say) 10 cm spacing can be effective for display purposes.

STRATEGIES USED IN THIS CHAPTER

- setting tasks in contexts which allow some students to work on simple examples and others to work on complex examples, possibly generalizing;
- using equipment to represent a mathematical concept;
- pooling collective knowledge;
- using linguistic and symbolic structures to aid description;
- asking students to 'write down' instead of putting hands up;
- choosing calculator, pencil-and-paper methods or pattern to generate answers, as appropriate;
- exploring using various tools to give different insights;
- using a tool (e.g. coordinate grid) for several different mathematical purposes to raise awareness of links in mathematics;
- using spatial patterns to develop understanding of number;
- recording and displaying work.

REFERENCES

Hart, K. (1981) *Children's Understanding of Number 11–16*. London: John Murray. This book contains a chapter on common problems in understanding fractions.

15

Summarizing inclusive mathematics

MATHEMATICS

Mathematics is a beautiful, creative, intriguing and imaginative subject. It has inspired people from all over the world and throughout history to study it. Mathematics also has the capacity to induce fear and panic. Many factors will determine whether students are inspired or fearful: how they are introduced to mathematics, how they are taught, how they are treated when they do not understand, what kind of atmosphere surrounds them while they are learning, how their own ideas can guide the direction of their work and so on. Teachers have a responsibility to create the kind of situation in which students, particularly those who enter secondary school with negative feelings about mathematics, can learn. Such situations may vary. For example, students react differently in practical, exploratory lessons and theoretical, abstract lessons; to problem solving methods and to algorithmic approaches. Some students feel safe when the work is very structured, while others prefer to explore their own way. A balance of approaches, providing a variety of ways to learn, is essential for effective learning. A key consideration, whatever the balance of teaching styles, is the atmosphere of the classroom: what it looks, sounds and feels like.

Teachers in schools cannot hope to replicate the atmosphere of, say, a family kitchen where mathematical problems are regularly discussed, nor of the reading corner of a library where a book-loving child can learn about the world. But a common feature of these and other environments in which good learners and good mathematicians are fostered is the sense of immersion in a supportive environment in which individual response is valued.

TEACHING MATHEMATICS TO ADOLESCENTS

Teaching adolescents anything is a challenge. It is a serious challenge to teach thirty of them simultaneously whilst competing with a plethora of outside influences. Their emotions are often awry, yet pressure is on them to engage with trigonometry, Hamlet and the chemical reaction between hydrochloric acid and sodium hydroxide sometimes within a couple of hours! Additionally they may have had no breakfast and have stocked up on snack foods at break. In order to achieve miracles, teachers have to learn about working with adolescents, structuring lessons, disciplinary issues, organizing classroom experiences, discriminating between purposeful and distracting noise and so on. When teachers put this learning into practice and are capable of creating harmonious working relationships based upon trust, understanding and mutual respect then it does become possible to teach a class of adolescents anything, but rarely can this be achieved quickly. For us, the most successful approach has always been to work *with* the conflicting influences on adolescents, and not to ignore them or work against them.

TEACHING MATHEMATICS IN INCLUSIVE CLASSROOMS

The central feature of this book is teaching mathematics to adolescents in inclusive classrooms, where students are not categorized by a measure of their 'ability' and separated into teaching groups accordingly. We have raised questions about the methods, reasons and assessments which are used to classify students. We have also challenged a common perception of hierarchy in mathematics which almost forces teachers to separate learners in order to follow prescribed pathways. Teaching inclusive groups is firmly grounded in equality and social justice; it is about raising standards of teaching and learning for all. Rising to this challenge, raising standards in mathematics classrooms while retaining interest, intrigue and creativity in mathematics is a fundamental concern in this book.

INTERACTING MATHEMATICALLY

We learn by asking questions and questioning answers, through observation and discussion. We teach by helping students ask questions and question answers, to conjecture about, and discuss, the phenomena they observe. The art of teaching is most clearly seen when the teacher interacts with individuals, small groups and whole classes. It is in these interactions that the teacher's thinking and planning come to fruition, and the nature of them influences how the students will see mathematics, and themselves as mathematicians. Each situation demands different skills and different forms of response.

Sometimes the teacher expects a student to answer questions and at other times the teacher will need to answer the student's questions, perhaps by posing a further question or by offering a direct answer. In the midst of teaching, decisions are made about how the language of mathematics is used to reveal mathematical meaning and how much telling the teacher does. The art of teaching includes improving the quality of mathematical interactions with students.

STRUCTURE AND INTERCONNECTEDNESS

Mapping a curriculum in which concepts are interconnected, linked by common skills or structures, can be a fascinating task. Exercises such as listing mathematical topics which involve multiplying a number by itself; identifying quadratic forms in various mathematical contexts; finding out where the distributive law is important, and so on, allow teachers to take professional responsibility for structuring a scheme of work and observing students' progression within it. Even with a given textbook which 'has to be covered', it is possible to take such responsibility. Even within an imposed curriculum it is possible to make and exploit such links.

SHARING TEACHING APPROACHES

When teachers work as a team their lesson ideas can be analysed so the whole team can learn more about how lessons can be started, what teaching strategies can be used, how the environment and resources are used, what questions can be asked of whom, how mathematical work can develop from the starting point, and what the resulting activities of the students are likely to be. Sharing such ideas is a key part of ongoing professional development in a mathematics team. Even when other matters crowd in and take up time, it is worth keeping space to discuss mathematics teaching, because it gives time for each teacher to be valued and respected by colleagues, and makes available ideas which may create a more rewarding, or easier, work environment.

ASSESSMENT

Assessment has a profound effect on students. Teachers make far-reaching decisions about students years before their eventual school-leaving achievements. Such decisions have to be wisely made. We have looked at the kinds of information collated, and the range of assessment tools used, some of which might give contrasting information about the same student. Judgements about students cannot be avoided, but awareness of possible bias, or the frailty of human judgement, and avoidance of irrevocability are crucial elements of professional decision-making.

Assessment also has a profound effect on teachers and the curriculum. The way students will be tested has to be reflected and included in the way they are taught, otherwise the teacher is not giving students the opportunity to achieve in ways recognized by society. Flexible ways of teaching and learning are more likely to encompass a range of possible assessment approaches. A student who has learned to see all mathematical questions as tasks to be interpreted, explored and evaluated is more likely to work imaginatively with assessment questions than one who has been taught to use certain cues to trigger algorithmic responses.

MATHEMATICAL TOPICS

We have grounded the early chapters of the book in our experience of teaching, and used examples from mathematics to illustrate our ideas. Nevertheless, it might still be possible to accuse us of being unrealistic. For this reason, we finished the book with several chapters showing treatments of core secondary mathematical topics which have been tried and tested in mixed-ability classes, sometimes including students with moderate and specific learning difficulties. As we have said several times, the ideas which lead to a 'good' lesson for one teacher do not necessarily create a worthwhile lesson for another. Our ideas are not recipes, but illustrations of how we, and others, have put beliefs about inclusivity into practice.

Index